Pope John Paul II spends a quiet moment in his private chapel.

Inside the
Vatican

By Bart McDowell

Photographed by James L. Stanfield

Prepared by the Book Division
National Geographic Society, Washington, D. C.

Onlookers applaud the Pope as he leaves a Roman church after a Sunday visit.
PRECEDING PAGES: A full moon rises over the dome of St. Peter's Basilica.
FOLLOWING PAGES: Altar boys cross St. Peter's Square on Epiphany morning.

Contents

*P*ope Benedict XVI (below) wears a red cappello romano, *a wide-brimmed hat for outdoor use. Rarely used by John Paul II, the hat is commonly known in Italian as a* saturno *because it reminds people of the planet Saturn. The Holy Father (right) greets a little boy at a general audience in Spain. Pope Benedict visited the* predominantly Catholic nation in November 2010. While there, he stressed the importance of the faith's deep roots in Spain, adding that these roots have helped to build a more decent society today.*

PRECEDING PAGES: John Paul II addresses the crowd in St. Peter's Square from the basilica's balcony on Easter Sunday 1991. To make this picture, photographer Jim Stanfield had to paint a camera gray to blend in, mount it high on a massive column, and test it to everyone's satisfaction. A last-minute hitch threatened the yearlong effort—a curtain blocked his view of the balcony, so a bishop had to step in to cue Jim when to take the photos.*

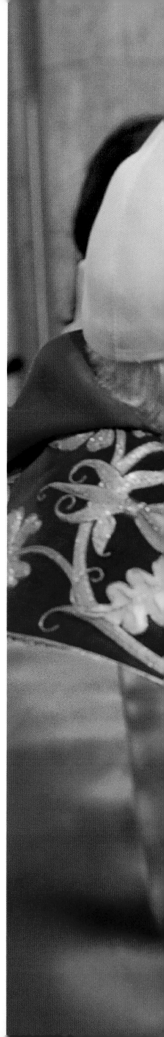

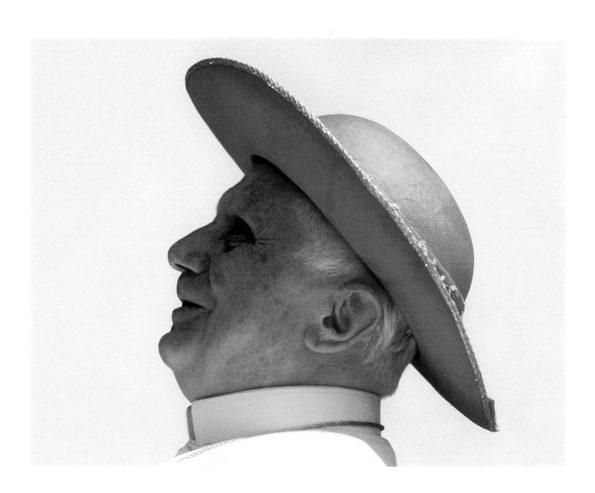

Foreword

This book has evolved as friendships do, with interest, followed by familiarity and respect. For five years, it had been my dream to cover the Vatican, the extraordinary community that is the world's smallest nation, the seat of the Roman Catholic Church, and an unparalleled repository of art and architecture. As a photographer, I wanted to capture the human side of this age-old institution.

I began my work in the Vatican with the disadvantage of being an outsider, unfamiliar with the complexities of the city-state and even of Catholicism. Early on, I was told that patience was essential to gain my behind-the-scenes coverage.

For nearly a year, I never missed a general papal audience or a public Mass. I frequently wrote letters to the Pope's secretary asking to photograph the Holy Father in settings rarely shown—his private elevator, chapel, and apartments. My requests brought no response. I sent color prints from my latest takes to those who had helped me, so that they could become familiar with my work. Little by little, Vatican officials started taking notice of my perseverance.

Three months before my deadline, the obstacles faded, and my presence at Vatican events began to be accepted. I was invited to cover private audiences with visiting dignitaries. Swiss Guards let me know about band rehearsals and family birthday parties. After Mass, when the Pope would wade into the crowd, Vatican police would steer me backward by pulling on my belt loops, thus permitting me to photograph the Holy Father without looking up from my viewfinder.

Eventually the Pope became aware of the *amerykański* photographer who wanted to "do things differently" and who "used a lot of film." His secretary started replying to my letters. "Be at the bronze doors at 6:30 a.m.," he would say, referring to the gateway to the papal palace. Such invitations allowed me to witness the Holy Father strolling in his gardens, embracing Polish President Lech Walesa, and in other intimate moments seldom shared with the outside world.

Looking back, patience was indeed the key, along with luck and persistence. With the help of many insiders who have since become close friends, and with the blessings of Pope John Paul II, I was given the rare opportunity to lift the veil of privacy for a privileged look inside the Vatican.

—*James L. Stanfield*

Pastor of the world's largest religious body, Pope John Paul II incenses an altar at Mass.

A Place Like No Other

We have come to St. Peter's Basilica to witness the canonization of a saint. Television lights illuminate Bernini's bronze canopy above the high altar, accenting the purple of bishops and the red of cardinals. The Pope, wearing white liturgical vestments and sitting on a cathedra of gold and white, reflects the full dazzle of a broadcast moment. He and we listen to the scriptural lesson:

> "There is one thing, my friends, that you must never
> forget: that with the Lord, 'a day' can mean a
> thousand years, and a thousand years is like a day.
> The Lord is not being slow to carry out his promises,
> as anybody else might be called slow; but he is being
> patient with you all. . . ."

These are the words of Simon Peter, fisherman, fisher of men, Christian Apostle in pagan Rome, rock of the church. By Peter's reckoning, God's days and man's millennia mingle here in a place that transcends time. Hours or centuries ago, gnarled old Michelangelo stood in rubble where we gather now, contemplating the still-unbuilt, sky-size dome above us. Before him by minutes or eras, the kneeling Charlemagne received his crown as Holy Roman Emperor. And later, troops of his imperial successor, Charles V, reddened this place with the blood of its defenders.

We are now visiting, by turn and at once, Nero's orgiastic circus, a sanctuary for saints, a temporal pawn of war, a goal of medieval pilgrims, and the center of the world's largest religious body, the Roman Catholic Church.

"The Italian word for this viewpoint," a young seminarian has told me, "is *romanitá*. The Roman way of looking at centuries instead of sound bites."

Some 16 feet directly beneath this altar where Pope John Paul II now

Above the high altar of St. Peter's Basilica, Bernini's baldachino, or canopy, rises on twisted columns toward the dome designed by Michelangelo. The Apostle's grave lies deep below the altar, beneath the lighted mosaic of Christ.

presides lie St. Peter's earthly remains, or so believes a host of cautious clergymen. I am inclined to also believe it, although I am a votary of St. Thomas the Doubter, a convinced Christian but not a Roman Catholic.

Time was when noncommunicants like me had uncertain access to the people of this holy place. Some of us were put to death as harshly as we returned such favors. No more. The methods of the Sacred Inquisition, or Holy Office, which once fiercely guarded the purity of the faith, have changed as utterly as its name, now the Congregation for the Doctrine of the Faith. The Index of Forbidden Books is a dusty bibliography consigned to history. The Pontifical Council for Promoting Christian Unity and the Pontifical Council for Interreligious Dialogue extend hospitable hands to other Christians, to Jews, Muslims, Buddhists, and followers of many other faiths.

But here, under television lights, we are witnessing the canonization of one of the church's own: the beatified, now about-to-be-called Saint Marie Marguerite d'Youville. Some of us—those able to move our eyes from the pageant to our programs—can read the story of this remarkable woman, born in Varennes, Quebec, in 1701. She had a hard, impoverished life. Still in her 20s, she had buried her husband and four of her six children. Yet she managed to educate her sons and to found the Sisters of Charity of Montreal, known as the Grey Nuns. Throughout her 70 years, she worked for the poor. In 1959, she was beatified by Pope John XXIII. "The power of Marguerite's intercession before God," relates our program, "was clearly evidenced when a young woman stricken with acute myeloblastic leukemia in 1978 was miraculously cured. This great favor opened for Marguerite the door to the official proclamation of sainthood." She thus becomes the first Canadian-born saint.

Some 3,000 of Marguerite's fellow Canadians have journeyed to Rome for this event, many of them her own Grey Nuns. Near them sit the diplomats accredited to the Holy See; the men wear white tie and tails. Their costumes are bright with medals and other decorations.

The liturgy proceeds. In Latin the Pontiff intones: *"Ad honorem Sanctae et Individuae Trinitatis . . . To the honor of the Holy and Indivisible Trinity, to the exaltation of the catholic faith . . . by the authority of Our Lord Jesus Christ . . . we decree and declare the Blessed Marie Marguerite d'Youville to be a Saint."*

PRECEDING PAGES: *Dominated by the basilica, the State of Vatican City forms an enclave in Rome west of the Tiber. The twin arms of Bernini's colonnade embrace St. Peter's Square; at its center stands an obelisk from ancient Egypt.*

The service continues, overlong, perhaps, for many non-Canadians. Youngsters fidget, an oldster nods off, a Grey Nun brings a handkerchief to her face to blot away tears, the proper diplomats sit unblinkingly erect.

In long lines, laity wait their turn to climb the seven steps to the high altar. Before the seated Pontiff, each visitor offers a religious object for blessing or a gift for the Holy Father. A middle-aged couple try to stay in step and kneel in unison before the cathedra; a lone woman moves with self-conscious care; a young man walks woodenly, tensed with the moment's honor. The line of pilgrims is ample.

But after the Eucharist, and after the music of the recessional has yielded to a hum of conversation, it is the petite, energetic Superior General of the Order of Grey Nuns, Sister Marguerite Letourneau, who clarifies the subject for me. "Canada has many, many saints," she says. "This is merely our first *acknowledged* saint." Her beatific smile could convince the devil himself.

*W*ithin this basilica, the largest church in Christendom, we have seen many of the citizens of the world's least populous nation. The Vatican, officially the State of Vatican City, is the territorial base of the Holy See. (A see is a diocese, from the Latin *sedes*—seat.) To Roman Catholics, the Holy See is primarily the diocese of Rome, presided over by its bishop, the pope, but the meaning has widened to include the central government of the church. The Vatican counts 416 citizens as of this moment, including 46 curial cardinals, 89 Swiss Guards, the 201 bearers of Vatican diplomatic passports, and a scattering of other residents, including the Pope himself. But no one in this small nation is considered a foreigner: In the specialness of the place, the very word "foreign" is foreign.

The United Nations has declared the Vatican a World Heritage site for its extraordinary cultural importance, thus entitling it to special protection. No other country has been so designated.

In the eyes of church officials, the primary purpose of the Vatican state today is to provide political independence to the pope as head of the Catholic Church. As an independent sovereign, he is subject to no government or political power.

"In international law," notes Alfons Cardinal Stickler, an authority on canon law, "the Holy See enjoys a sovereignty distinct from the territory of the Vatican city-state." Thus it is the Holy See with its 906 million worldwide adherents, not the city-state, that enjoys diplomatic relations with 123 countries.

The Vatican has no privately owned real estate, no income taxes, and no general elections. Its borders require no passport, merely an identification.

For all its visible history, the Vatican as we know it now dates only from 1929 and the Lateran Treaty between the Holy See and Italy. The borders of the city-state were clearly defined, a plot of real estate "just big enough to keep body and soul together," as Pope Pius XI described it: 108.7 acres in a trapezium shape, completely walled except for the great open space facing St. Peter's Square. The area of the entire Vatican is smaller than the grounds of the U.S. Capitol in Washington, D.C., about one-fourth the size of Monaco, one-eighth as big as New York City's Central Park. Guides frequently remark that "you can walk all the way around Vatican City in 40 minutes."

But lest the space seem confining, the Holy See has sovereignty over about a dozen other buildings beyond the Vatican walls, conveyed through the Lateran Treaty and later understandings with the Italian government. They include the papal summer residence—Castel Gandolfo—and the basilicas of St. John Lateran, St. Paul's Outside-the-Walls, and Santa Maria Maggiore.

Small as it is, the city-state sponsors a bureaucracy. Pope John XXIII was once asked how many people work in the Vatican.

"About half of them," he replied.

A bit more literally, some 4,000 people are employed by the Vatican. Official office hours seem enviable, but overtime is prodigious. The clergy and lay employees write reports in dozens of languages and concern themselves with birth, death, and immortal souls, with budgets, armaments, and angels, with poverty, prisons, schools, saints, and the exploding universe. They also preserve some of the world's great collections of art, books, and documents. And as they go about their daily chores, these people of the Vatican—whether curators, cooks, or cardinals—make up a community unique in the world.

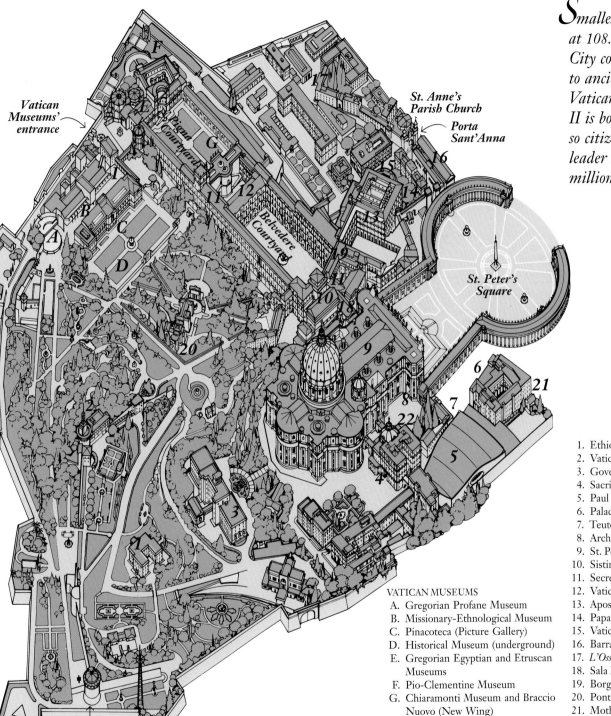

Vatican Museums' entrance

Vatican Museums' entrance

St. Anne's Parish Church

Porta Sant'Anna

Pagna Courtyard

Belvedere Courtyard

St. Peter's Square

St. John's Tower

Heliport

Smallest state in the world at 108.7 acres, Vatican City covers an area known to ancient Romans as Vaticanus. Pope John Paul II is both ruler of its 400 or so citizens and spiritual leader of the world's 906 million Roman Catholics.

1. Ethiopian College
2. Vatican Radio
3. Government Palace
4. Sacristy and Treasury
5. Paul VI Audience Hall
6. Palace of the Holy Office
7. Teutonic College
8. Arch of the Bells
9. St. Peter's Basilica
10. Sistine Chapel
11. Secret Archives
12. Vatican Apostolic Library
13. Apostolic Palace
14. Papal apartments
15. Vatican bank
16. Barracks of the Swiss Guard
17. *L'Osservatore Romano* offices
18. Sala Regia (Royal Hall)
19. Borgia Apartments
20. Pontifical Academy of Sciences
21. Mother Teresa's hospice
22. Square of the First Christian Martyrs

VATICAN MUSEUMS

A. Gregorian Profane Museum
B. Missionary-Ethnological Museum
C. Pinacoteca (Picture Gallery)
D. Historical Museum (underground)
E. Gregorian Egyptian and Etruscan Museums
F. Pio-Clementine Museum
G. Chiaramonti Museum and Braccio Nuovo (New Wing)
H. Collection of Modern Religious Art
I. Pio-Christian Museum

Rare snowfall dusts St. Peter's Square on Epiphany, the January 6 feast day celebrating the wise men's homage to the Christ child. Huddled against the storm, worshipers leaving Mass pass a Christmas tree and a shed holding a Nativity scene.
Behind the crowd rises St. Peter's 17th-century facade, by Maderno, topped by statues of Christ, John the Baptist, and the Apostles. On special holidays, throngs of up to a quarter of a million people fill the piazza.

*S*wapping pleasantries, two cardinals prepare to enter the Synod Hall for a consistory, an assembly of cardinals that advises the pope. Such meetings supplement the work of the curia—an administrative body made up of congregations, councils, an commissions—in helping the pope govern the Ron Catholic Church.

*B*eyond the illuminated statuary of Bernini's colonnade, lights from the Pope's private offices glow long after dark descends on the Vatican. Below, a Swiss Guard stands watch at Bernini's bronze doors, main entrance to the Apostolic Palace and the papal apartments.

A young Polish girl prays in anticipation of receiving Pope John Paul II's blessing. Her intensity of prayer at such a young age touched me.

A follower whispers into the Pope's ear at an audience in St. Peter's Square. People loved to get close to the Pontiff, and I noticed he always listened attentively to what they had to say.

Faces of the Faithful

LOOKING BACK ON MY COVERAGE of papal audiences, I'm reminded of the deep love John Paul II's followers felt for him. Young and old behaved as if this was the most exciting day of their lives.

People would spontaneously break out in cheers when he appeared—many waving colorful banners, others gazing devotedly, some deep in prayer. I could sense the affection they had for the Pope, their intense desire to get a glimpse of him and receive his blessing.

I wanted to capture the depth of their passion in photographs. Their faces, filled with reverence and celebration, became the way to do so. Some faces were weathered with the trials and tribulations of life; others were unlined and angelic, their lives still largely ahead of them. In every case, expressive eyes revealed the intensity of their emotions as they experienced the presence of their spiritual leader.

Each week, a handful of public papal audiences took place where visitors— and I—could experience the Pope's presence firsthand. One of my favorites was the Angelus, a Sunday devotion where the Holy Father appeared at the window of his chambers to bless the people in St. Peter's Square. The ringing of the bell of St. Peter's Basilica meant the noon prayer was about to begin. Crowds anticipating his arrival were always in a festive mood. The bay window of the papal chambers would open—a crimson tapestry decorated with the Pope's coat of arms hanging from the sill—and John Paul would appear at the window of his fourth-floor study. The gathered crowd inevitably erupted in applause.

He also addressed thousands of people at Wednesday audiences, either in St. Peter's Square or the Pope Paul VI Audience Hall. After celebrating Mass, John Paul often approached the assembled group, warmly greeting anyone within reach—shaking hands and kissing babies, embracing young and old. People clamored to get as close to him as possible.

Whatever the venue, I witnessed the growing glow on the faces of the faithful as they watched and listened. People gazed devoutly at him, their faces filled with prayerful expressions of joy and peace, and I was struck by the spiritual connection he had with his devoted followers. It seemed to me that the hearts of these pilgrims were dancing, and I found myself getting caught up in the fervor. It was impossible not to. Pope John Paul II made my heart dance too.

—James L. Stanfield

Nuns and schoolchildren cheer and wave banners in St. Peter's Square as the Pope appears on the balcony of his study to bless a walking marathon for the students. Time after time, I would marvel at the thousands of people who would gather in the enormous square for papal appearances such as this.

A nun gazes devotedly toward the papal balcony as the Holy Father addresses the crowd in St. Peter's Square. Audiences provided wonderful opportunities to see the Pope interact with his followers.

The Pope blesses a disabled woman in St. Peter's Square during an audience for people with physical challenges. John Paul II felt a particular affection for those who had special needs.

The Legacy of Peter

No commercial tours take visitors into the archaeological excavations beneath St. Peter's Basilica. But small, family-size groups are permitted now and again with a knowledgeable guide. They make their way down cramped stairways and along low, narrow tunnels that burrow through layers of Roman history.

Our group of eight had a curious bit of luck: Without warning, the electricity failed, and we found ourselves blind in the darkness. One woman whispered to her husband; otherwise we were as quiet as the second-century tombs around us. We could feel the weight of St. Peter's and the burden of its very age. Time had paused. Then our guide, a young seminarian from Alabama, turned on his flashlight and continued his disquisition. But we had briefly tasted the darkness of those centuries . . . before a Pope's death in February 1939 brought light and labor to these parts.

The Pope was Pius XI. Shortly after his burial in a grotto beneath the basilica, architects and conservators decided to proceed with a long-standing project: to convert the grottoes into an underground chapel. It was slow, heavy work with shovel and crowbar, removing pavement, digging into the hardpacked earth and detritus below.

Almost at once the workers found burial sites and sarcophagi. No one was surprised; every Roman had heard that this had been an old cemetery.

And then one day a workman on the south aisle struck something that seemed to be the top of a brick wall—terracotta on one side, plaster on the other, and colored a kind of turquoise. More of the surrounding dirt was removed, until the men could see that brick walls more than a foot thick defined a quadrangle some 20 feet long. This had once been a building, its roof long ago removed, and its interior filled with earth.

Caravaggio's dramatic painting shows St. Peter being crucified head down. Tradition holds that the Apostle felt unworthy to hang upright as Christ did. Near the reputed spot in Rome, a great basilica would rise in Peter's name.

Years later, Carlo Pietrangeli, Director General of the Pontifical Monuments, Museums, and Galleries, would compare the area beneath St. Peter's to Pompeii or Herculaneum, where "the eruption of Vesuvius suddenly sealed the city beneath a layer of stones and ash." On Vatican Hill, however, it was the haste of the fourth-century builders of St. Peter's, who buried the old cemetery on orders from Emperor Constantine. The fill-dirt protected old tombs from grave robbers and weather.

Carefully, the excavators removed the dirt until they saw that the plastered wall had an arrangement of niches for cremation urns like those used in pagan Rome. Soon they found a red panel with a picture of a partridge, various stucco figures, paintings of flowers and fruit, even a rural scene showing an ox and a ram, and then some Christian symbols: a woman drawing water from a well and doves with an olive branch. Finally, on a marble slab laid into the floor, they saw the Latin words *dormit in pace*—rests in peace. This was the grave of a Christian.

An inscription on the marble slab identified the Christian as a woman named Aemilia Gorgonia. Her grieving husband had composed a eulogy to her beauty and goodness ("sweet-souled Gorgonia," he called her). She had died young: Her age was meticulously recorded as 28 years, 2 months, and 28 days. Scholars were excited. They had come upon a tomb remarkably well preserved, dating from the days of Rome's greatest splendor, around A.D. 150. Nearby, the excavators found the remains of a woman wearing gold jewelry and the residue of cloth dyed royal purple. Another stone inscription identified the director of a troupe of actors, a man praised for his musical talent.

Meanwhile, diggers were finding other graves outside the walls of the first tomb. The site promised to become one of the great archaeological resources of the century. With the permission of the new Pope, Pius XII, a team of four specialists from the Papal Institute for Christian Archaeology began more extensive work under the leadership of the administrator of St. Peter's Basilica.

Though only one member of the team was a trained archaeologist, all were conscientious about their responsibilities. They took careful notes and ensured that human bones were conserved for later reburial. The site beneath the basilica's high altar received special care. Tradition had forever held that the remains of Simon Peter himself rested beneath it.

PRECEDING PAGES: Sculptured in marble by Bernini, Roman Emperor Constantine appears awed by the vision of a cross presaging victory in A.D. 312. Constantine legalized Christianity and founded the first St. Peter's Basilica.

Excavators were uncovering a rich assortment of ancient art—frescoes, an early Christian mosaic, statues—as well as graves easily identified as Christian. Other graves represented a syncretic hodgepodge of cults: dancing satyrs, maenads, deities ranging from Apollo to Isis. "Romans of those days took no chances," one priest observes.

Soon the excavators had logged and studied nearly 20 mausoleums. Groups of historians and archivists were combing through the earliest records to learn more about the Vaticanus, the ancient area of marshy valley and hills on the west bank of the Tiber from which the Vatican takes its name. The historian Tacitus called it infamous for malaria; scholarly Pliny the Elder dreaded its large snakes; and the poet Martial decried its vineyards for producing sour wine. Nevertheless, wealthy Romans built villas with extensive gardens there, and, in the middle of the first century, a bridge went up across the Tiber to connect the Vaticanus to Rome.

It was in the Vaticanus in A.D. 40 that the deranged Emperor Caligula began to build the circus that Nero finished. Caligula had a giant obelisk brought from Egypt to mark the center of his circus. It stood until 1586 near what is now the south wall of St. Peter's, clearly identifying the site.

*H*istory and tradition intertwine at this point. When Rome burned in A.D. 64, Nero blamed the obscure sect of Christians, arrested many of them, and brought them to his circus. Some he threw to wild beasts. Others were burned alive, reported Tacitus, "so as to serve the purpose of lamps when daylight failed." Still others were crucified, among them the Apostle Peter, who, according to church tradition, was martyred, head down, *juxta obeliscum*—next to the obelisk. The same tradition had it that disciples took down Peter's body and buried it in a shallow grave in the cemetery that adjoined the circus. By the year 160, a simple shrine known as the Trophy of Gaius marked Peter's grave, a secret shared by the persecuted Christians. A red wall defined the upper part of the site.

By the fourth century a struggle was under way for mastery of the empire. In 312, the Emperor Constantine faced his rival Maxentius just outside Rome. The battle would decide his fate and Rome's. Later, Constantine told the historian

Eusebius about his experience: "He said that with his own eyes . . . while the day was already fading, he had seen a shining cross in the sky, more brilliant than the sun, accompanied by the words *In hoc signo vinces*—By this sign, thou shalt conquer. He remained stunned by the vision, and so did all the army following him in the expedition, which had also seen the miracle."

The battle was joined and won. Constantine gave full credit to the Christian God and at once decreed Christianity a lawful religion. He built a church in Rome on Lateran Hill, which came to be known as St. John Lateran, and presented it to Pope Militiades, along with a palace for a papal residence. (The title "pope"—from the Greek word *pappas*, father—was used for any bishop during the first centuries of the church.) To this day, St. John Lateran remains the cathedral church of the bishop of Rome, now the only Catholic bishop called pope.

Next, Constantine built a larger basilica across the Tiber on Vatican Hill, directly over the cemetery and the small shrine marking the grave of Peter, the first bishop of Rome and now viewed as the first Pope. To do this, he had the roofs of the mausoleums removed and the area filled with dirt. The large dimensions of the basilica reflected the needs of the "countless crowds come from all parts of the Roman Empire," as one eyewitness reported. Banquets and ceremonies were held there to honor St. Peter, and many Christians, including numerous popes, were buried beneath the floor.

Pilgrims needed shelter, of course, so hostels sprang up around the basilica known today as Old St. Peter's. By the sixth century, the popes had built two *episcopia* to house themselves and their retinues when they came from the Lateran for devotions. And with the movement of crowds and time, the church needed alterations. A new high altar was installed about 600, to be replaced twice more in the next thousand years.

Old St. Peter's and the buildings around it were still unfortified in 846, when a raiding party of some 10,000 Saracen pirates landed at Rome's port of Ostia and swept inland. Romans resisted behind their walls, but the basilica was seized, looted, and defiled, according to one chronicler, with "unspeakable iniquities."

As the modern excavations came closer to the area under the high altar, diggers encountered older graves. The work grew more sensitive and more tedious. And then they uncovered a wall painted red. At right angles to it stood another wall of pale, mottled blue; on its surface was a tangled, mostly illegible patchwork of graffiti. Beside these walls, the excavators found a cache of bones. They put them in a metal box, which was carried to the Pope's apartments and sealed.

Lips were also sealed and would remain so until the next Holy Year, 1950. As work continued, every measure of dirt was sifted for further evidence. Votive offerings were found. And coins—two thousand of them.

The red wall and the graffiti wall could be clearly identified as parts of the early grave site, but the garbled inscriptions and the bones needed further study. Rumors and published speculations whetted public curiosity, but the Vatican remained silent for another year. Then Pope Pius made his announcement by radio:

"Has the tomb of St. Peter really been found?" he began. "To that question the answer is beyond all doubt, *yes*. . . . A second question . . . refers to the relics of St. Peter. Have they been found? At the side of the tomb remains of human bones have been discovered. However, it is impossible to prove . . . that they belong to the body of the Apostle."

The Pope's caution was wise. The bones stored in the papal apartments proved to be those of several people—and of some domesticated animals as well. By reason of age and sex, none of those bones could have been Peter's.

*B*ut long after the death of Pius XII in 1958, the mystery continued. Other bones had been discovered in the graffiti wall and conserved in a storeroom. These bones were carefully analyzed in laboratories and pronounced those of a robust man between 60 and 70 years of age—a description that could fit St. Peter. But why had these bones not been logged in? The Catholic News Service has noted that the story of the excavation of the bones is one "of noble intentions marred in part by professional jealousies and gaps of information."

The laboratory analysis at least persuaded the cautious Pope Paul VI. In June 1968, he announced that "the relics of St. Peter have been identified in a manner which we believe convincing." The Pope then returned the bones to their resting place in the grafitti wall. This time, they remained visible behind glass.

Since then, no further excavations have been made or planned beneath St.

Peter's. Visitors can retrace the progress of those earlier underground explorations, descending into other times, viewing the tombs in a pale, crepuscular light designed to keep antique pigments from fading. Glass panels protect the mausoleums, giving them the unreal ambience of aquariums. And yet the sculptures and pictures evoke the fears, hopes, and consolations of grieving survivors. A likeness of Bacchus celebrates the joy of drunkenness in the next world . . . a peacock stands as a preening talisman of life after death . . . ripples of water make a metaphor for life's continuity, an amniotic River Styx.

We feel closer, of course, to the dead whose beliefs were more like our own, to sweet-souled Gorgonia, perhaps, and her furtive fellow worshipers. For myself, as I view the glass-shielded bones of Simon Peter—or of a man much like him—I feel a kind of gratitude for the confusion and debate still going on. They leave us all room to doubt, to wonder at the lasting mysteries of Peter's life and death, and to remember that the remains of this sturdy fisherman endure not so much in a grave as in the human heart.

H. G. Wells gives this advice: "It is on the whole more convenient to keep history and theology apart."

True. And here we must be selective with our temporal history, for we are mostly concerned with just one place—the piece of earth now enclosed by the Vatican walls.

For centuries, of course, no walls existed. In A.D. 330, Constantine moved the capital of the Roman Empire east to Constantinople. Invasions by Germanic tribes and squabbles among local barons threw Italy into chaos. The popes restored public order and provided public services; in the process, they added considerably to their temporal powers. For the next centuries, they would be much concerned with statecraft, armies, and alliances.

Outstanding in the medieval world was Pope Gregory I, known as Gregory the Great. Scholar, teacher, writer, administrator, Gregory enormously enhanced the papacy's prestige and authority. In his quest to bring peace, he became virtually the ruler of Italy in the late sixth century. He reorganized the vast church-owned lands throughout the peninsula, laying the foundation for an independent papal state that would endure for more than a thousand years and turn the popes into de facto political rulers.

It was not until after the Saracens pillaged Old St. Peter's in 846 that steps were taken to secure it. Pope Leo IV encircled the basilica and the adjacent Borgo neighborhood with towering battlements and a wall some 40 feet high. In June 852, the fortified Vatican settlement became officially the Leonine City, an urban entity separate from Rome. Through the years, other popes extended the walls and enlarged the boundaries of the city.

Such was the mystical allure of the church in Rome that Frankish king Charlemagne came several times to the city. On Christmas Day in the year 800, he was crowned in Old St. Peter's as emperor of a new Holy Roman Empire. He was the first of a long line of European rulers who would travel to the basilica to receive their crowns from papal hands.

Some had to bring their armies. Popes and rulers clashed continuously over the right to invest bishops and influence church affairs. When Henry IV, the German king and Holy Roman Emperor-designate, collided with the great reformer Gregory VII, the Pope deposed and excommunicated the king. Henry seized Rome in 1084 and drove Pope Gregory into exile. He had himself crowned in St. Peter's by a prelate of his own choosing, an antipope, as a pretender to the papal throne is called.

Henry's son and successor, Henry V, also quarreled with the church over the right to invest bishops. In 1111, he forced Pope Paschal II, under threat of deposition, to crown him emperor in St. Peter's.

Over the next two centuries, the popes tried to increase their political power to protect the freedom of the church. The influential Innocent III saw his spiritual position as "set midway between God and man, below God but above man." Other popes went further. In 1302, Boniface VIII asserted the church's supremacy: "There are two swords, the one to be wielded . . . by priests, the other by kings and soldiers, but by the will and permission of the priest." King Philip IV of France charged Boniface with an array of sins and tried to run him out of office.

When a French cleric became Pope Clement V in 1305, the prestige of the papacy continued to sink. Following his coronation at Lyons, Clement bowed to the wishes of King Philip and, in 1309, settled his court at Avignon. His successors, also French, built the Palace of the Popes beside the River Rhône—"the loveliest and vastest house on earth," a contemporary described it—to demonstrate Avignon's primacy to the world.

The 68-year "Babylonian Captivity" proved expensive in treasure, blood, and faith itself. The population of Rome reportedly dwindled to fewer than 17,000 souls; streets and houses were abandoned. The papal palace at St. John Lateran was destroyed by fire.

Finally, in 1377, Pope Gregory XI, fearing a takeover of the papal state, returned to Rome. With the Lateran palace gone, he settled on the Vatican as the official papal residence. But almost at once another disaster occurred. The papacy was split between Rome and Avignon, with two and—briefly—three popes, each excommunicating the others. The Great Western Schism lasted 39 years. It divided Christendom into different allegiances and nearly destroyed the church.

A general council met and, in 1417, ended the schism by electing a new Pope, Martin V. With Martin the Renaissance papacy began, an era that lasted well into the 16th century. This was a period of creative genius that turned the entire Vatican into a work of art. Nicholas V, a distinguished man of letters, brought the church into step with the Renaissance. In the mid-1400s, he had scores of churches, palaces, and bridges rebuilt, and hired outstanding artists to decorate them. Nicholas's successors—some of them scoundrels—included men with names such as della Rovere, Borgia, Medici.

What would you say about the worldly pontiffs of the Renaissance? I put this question one day to Father Leonard Boyle, director of the Vatican Library. He sighed long and deeply. "Well, of course, it's easy for us to judge them by our standards of today," he replied. "It's a little like watching old movies; we're amazed that everyone smokes all the time.

"But we should consider the way their contemporaries saw them. Were they part of the normal scene?"

The Renaissance scene was itself far from normal. Nation-states were still being sorted out. Individualism was fierce. Family loyalty meant everything. Spiritual values waned. The Vatican became highly secularized, as much a center of temporal government and international intrigue as the church's headquarters.

For some popes, the pursuit of power became an end in itself. Times were tumultuous; life was dangerous, cheap, and often brief.

"Yes, we had a grim batch of popes then," notes Monsignor Charles Burns, of the Vatican Secret Archives. "But these men were basically political."

Not all the Renaissance popes were bad. Pius II stands out as a humanist and for his crusading vision of a united Christian Europe. He had written novels and erotic comedies before taking holy orders. As Pope, he kept a kind of diary which he wrote in the third person. Of his coronation, he noted:

"Pope Pius II was crowned at Rome in St. Peter's September 3, in the year of our salvation 1458, and the same day he went in solemn procession to the Lateran, where he narrowly escaped death in the mob who fought with swords for the horse on which he had ridden. He was saved by the mercy of Heaven and . . . gave a royal banquet. . . ."

*L*ess than four decades later, a Spanish Borgia was elected Pope Alexander VI. Though greedy for the pleasures of women and gold and for the advancement of his illegitimate children, Alexander was also a lover of art. He left us the Vatican's magnificent Borgia Apartments, decorated by Pinturicchio. Julius II, known as *Il terribile*, a soldier as hard and sharp as his sword, was an even greater patron of the arts. In 1506, he laid the cornerstone for a new basilica to replace the dilapidated Old St. Peter's. The building would take 120 years to complete.

In 1513, a Medici prince succeeded Julius as Pope Leo X. Leo fought to keep Italy free of foreign domination and to extend his family's influence outside Florence. The wars and the rebuilding of St. Peter's were expensive, but Leo also spent recklessly on his pleasures. "God has given us the papacy," he reportedly said. "Let us enjoy it." His dinners featured such delicacies as peacocks' tongues, nightingales flying out of pies, and naked children climbing out of puddings. He soon found himself deeply in debt and paying high interest to nearly every banking house in Rome.

One way for the church to raise money was to grant indulgences in exchange for charitable donations. An indulgence is a pardon of time in purgatory for a sin

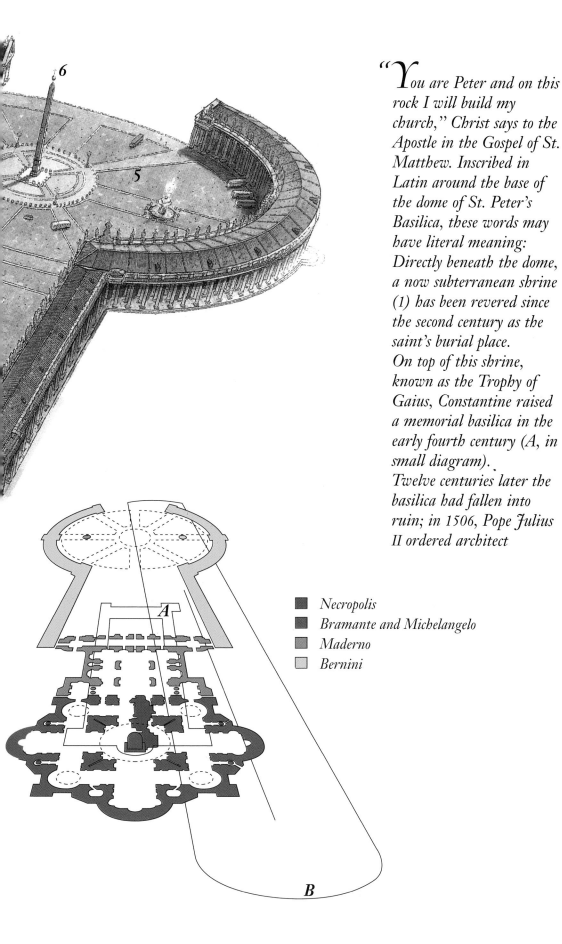

"You are Peter and on this rock I will build my church," Christ says to the Apostle in the Gospel of St. Matthew. Inscribed in Latin around the base of the dome of St. Peter's Basilica, these words may have literal meaning: Directly beneath the dome, a now subterranean shrine (1) has been revered since the second century as the saint's burial place.

On top of this shrine, known as the Trophy of Gaius, Constantine raised a memorial basilica in the early fourth century (A, in small diagram).

Twelve centuries later the basilica had fallen into ruin; in 1506, Pope Julius II ordered architect Bramante to demolish it and to plan a new basilica, which became a showcase for Renaissance and baroque art. Among the artists who worked on it over the next 170 years were Michelangelo, whose designs inspired the immense dome, capped by its lantern tower (2); Maderno, who built the portico and facade (3); and Bernini, whose creations include the "Throne of St. Peter" in the apse (4) and the colonnade that enfolds the piazza (5). Bridging the ages, a Christian cross tops the 82-foot Egyptian obelisk (6), moved here from its original site nearby: the Roman circus where St. Peter is supposed to have been crucified (B, in diagram).

- ■ Necropolis
- ■ Bramante and Michelangelo
- ■ Maderno
- ■ Bernini

that has been forgiven through penance. Some clergy of the 16th century took the practice too far: They preached that indulgences would remit the punishment due for future sins. In 1517, an Augustinian monk in Germany bitterly dissented.

"Out of love and zeal for truth . . . the following theses will be publicly discussed . . . under the chairmanship of the reverend father Martin Luther, Master of Arts and Sacred Theology." Thus began Luther's 95 Theses. "Any truly repentant Christian has a right to full remission of penalty and guilt, even without indulgence letters."

Prompted in part by the indulgence issue but deeply rooted in other causes, the Protestant Reformation had begun.

*T*he ambitions of the French and the Germans to dominate Italy—and Pope Clement VII's oscillating loyalties—brought Rome to ruin. In 1526, Clement formed an alliance with the French to check the expanding power of the Holy Roman Emperor, Charles V. On the morning of May 6, 1527, Charles's armies—Spanish Catholics and German Lutherans, commanded by the Constable of Bourbon—entered Rome. Within hours, Clement's defenses had collapsed. Swiss Guards heroically defended the person of the Pope; 147 of them died, thus buying time for Clement to take cover nearby inside the bulky fortress of Sant'Angelo.

"I ascended to the keep and at the same instant Pope Clement came in through the corridors into the castle." So reported swashbuckling Benvenuto Cellini, goldsmith, sculptor, artillery master, and unreliable memoirist. Cellini manned "five fine pieces of artillery on the highest point of the castle. . . . On one occasion the Pope was walking round the circular keep when he observed a Spanish Colonel . . . formerly in his service. . . . I fired, and hit my man exactly in the middle." The Spaniard was "cut in two fair halves. The Pope . . . derived great pleasure and amazement from the sight. . . . Upon my bended knees I then besought him to give me the pardon of his blessing for that homicide; and for all the others I had committed . . . in the service of the Church."

For five grotesque months, the Vatican and all Rome were occupied by the invaders. They looted palaces and churches. They auctioned off nuns, and raped and killed them. Hundreds of murdered citizens were thrown into the Tiber, and thousands of others were so badly buried that plague became epidemic.

The Pope stayed inside the Castel Sant'Angelo until December, when he was able to escape. He made up with Charles by paying a large indemnity and agreeing to allow German troops to be stationed on papal lands. In 1530, to seal the reconciliation, Pope Clement crowned Charles emperor — the last such papal ceremony for the Holy Roman Empire.

The church and the Eternal City were both rebuilt by the labors of many men. Certainly the wise and wily Pope Paul III brought large reforms; in 1545, he convened the Council of Trent to confront the challenge of Protestantism. Though it came too late to reestablish church unity and would not be implemented entirely for decades, the council laid the groundwork for far-reaching change within the church.

But perhaps the man who did the most in the shortest time was the "Iron Pope," Sixtus V. An ascetic Franciscan cardinal, he came to the papal conclave in 1585 as a retiree, bent with years, on crutches. Fellow cardinals, sure that his reign would be brief, elected him Pope. Therewith, he is supposed to have thrown down his crutches and announced, "Hitherto I have sought the key of heaven bent over: now I have found it." And he stood upright.

Sixtus reorganized the administration of the church, cut expenses dramatically (he himself continued to live in Franciscan poverty), stamped out banditry, drained marshes, and generally improved the lot of his subjects. He gave form to the new Rome as the center of a renewed church. Visitors today can see his urban plan painted on a wall in the reading room, or Great Hall, of the Vatican Library. The plan shows the work-in-progress, with vast avenues carved across the cityscape and a dozen Egyptian obelisks, each topped by a cross marking the vistas that would replace medieval clutter.

"And Sixtus V also built this part of the library," notes the director, Father Boyle. To do so, "Sixtus split the vast Belvedere Courtyard in two, putting a stop to the theatrical performances and occasional bullfights held there." The remaining area is now a parking lot for Vatican employees; considering the nature of Roman drivers, bullfights might have been milder.

Sixtus V used his days with severity. A man in a hurry, he was driven, driving, and unworried about popularity. When he died after only five years in office, a festive Roman mob tore down his statue. But Roman mobs rarely rewarded virtue. When the reformer Hadrian VI passed from this world in 1523, Romans placed garlands of flowers at the door of his bungling physician.

By the 17th century, the papal state had begun a political and economic decline, diminishing the pope's temporal authority. Nationalism was on the rise in Europe, and Roman Catholicism now only one faith among several. European rulers insisted the popes not interfere in their business, while maintaining the right to intervene in church affairs.

For the next two centuries, this power struggle put church and state on collision courses. Four times the papal government was overthrown. First, in 1798, following the French Revolution, French troops proclaimed a Roman Republic and captured Pope Pius VI, who died a prisoner in France. Then, in 1808, Napoleon dismantled the papal state and took Pius VII prisoner. And in 1849, at the start of the long reign of Pius IX, the Italians announced a second Roman Republic. French troops helped restore Pius IX. But by 1870 Italian troops had occupied the papal lands and proclaimed Rome the capital of the new kingdom of Italy.

The new Italian government enacted laws that permitted the Pope to use the Vatican and other properties considered part of the kingdom. But Pius IX refused to accept this new status. He regarded the Holy See as a sacred trust to be handed over to his successor in the same condition it had been received. He and his immediate successors chose to live as "prisoners in the Vatican," never setting foot outside the grounds from the moment of their election, and forbidding Catholics from taking part in the "usurping kingdom of Italy."

It was not until 1929 that Pius XI, in negotiating the Lateran Treaty, recognized Italy as a kingdom and Rome as its capital. In return, the Italian government indemnified the church for loss of the papal state and recognized the independence of the State of Vatican City, bringing the centuries of bitter conflict at last to an end. Ironically, it was only then, with all political power stripped away, that true papal independence was won.

Pagan and Christian symbols blend in a ceiling mosaic known as Christ Helios—Christ the Sun—in the ancient necropolis beneath St. Peter's. The Apollo-like figure ascends in a chariot; light rays around his head suggest a cross.

*I*n the second-century cemetery excavated under the basilica in 1939, workers uncovered scallop-shell wall niches, some still holding cremation urns, and numerous other pagan burial sites, including that of Caetennius Antigonus, whose family memorial stands at center (right). A marble slab in the floor marked a Christian grave, that of Aemilia Gorgonia, who died at the age of 28. Among its decorations was a woman drawing water, a Christian symbol of the refreshment the spirit might expect in heaven. Bones now displayed in the graffiti wall (below), near the second-century shrine to St. Peter, are believed by some to be the Apostle's. Cryptic markings on the wall may refer to Peter.

Originally the tomb of Emperor Hadrian, Castel Sant'Angelo sheltered more than one pope fleeing attack on the Vatican. In 1084, Pope Gregory VII took refuge there after clashing with German King Henry IV over the right to invest bishops. While Gregory held out in the medieval fortress, a pretender, or antipope, crowned Henry emperor in St. Peter's.

FOLLOWING PAGES: Swathed in scarlet, the College of Cardinals gathers to hear Pope John Paul II appoint 28 new members to its ranks. Organized in the 11th century, the college advises the pope and, on his death, elects a successor.

*P*ope Gregory XI blesses the crowd gathered in front of the old Constantinian basilica in 1377. Giorgio Vasari's 16th-century painting depicts Gregory's return from Avignon, in France, where popes had held court for 68 years. After his death, a bitter 39-year schism ensued, with rival popes in Rome and Avignon, and a thira, briefly, in Pisa.

With the restoration in 1417 of a single pope in Rome, Renaissance pontiffs such as the worldly Borgia Alexander VI (below, in a detail from a Pinturicchio painting) sponsored a dazzling era of art and learning.

FOLLOWING PAGES: From the Renaissance purity of the pilasters to the baroque splendor of the altar canopy, St. Peter's reflects the period of greatest artistic creativity at the Vatican.

*S*hrewd diplomat, Pope Paul III gazes from Titian's lifelike portrait. In 1545, he convened the Council of Trent to rid the church of abuses and to clarify its doctrine, hoping to prevent further defections to the Protestant Reformation. Like much of Germany, England under King Henry VIII had already broken with Rome. After Pope Clement VII denied his 1530 petition for a marriage annulment— shown at right with the seals of 85 members of the English clergy, nobility, and gentry—King Henry declared himself head of the new Church of England.

Richly frescoed, the Sistine Hall of the Vatican Library glorifies writing and the reign of Pope Sixtus V. In 1587, Sixtus commissioned Domenico Fontana to build a new wing to house the library's overflowing collections. Four master painters and a hundred assistants completed the frescoes in just 13 months. Today, the library's collections include about 150,000 manuscripts and more than two million books, some of which are on view in this display area.

FOLLOWING PAGES: Finishing touch of a master, Bernini's fountain in St. Peter's Square sets off the dramatic sweep of his colonnade—all built during the 17th-century reign of one of the great patrons of baroque art, Pope Alexander VII.

The Concordat of 1801 (left) between Pope Pius VII and Napoleon Bonaparte established a precedent-setting relationship between the church and the modern state, in this case France. It would result in the surrender of most papal lands by 1870. Pius IX, whose treasures include this ring and chalice, refused to cede temporal power over the Vatican and declared himself a prisoner there.

An eighth-century mosaic of Christ marks the grave site of the Apostle Peter in the necropolis under St. Peter's Basilica. Tucked beneath the high altar, the striking mosaic was almost hidden from sight,

Hidden Treasures

I KNEW THAT ST. PETER'S BASILICA was home to an incredible collection of art. However, I was surprised to discover that what appeared at first glance to be paintings were actually mosaics. In fact, mosaics make up nearly all the artwork in and around the basilica.

Two mosaics that are somewhat hidden from sight particularly caught my attention. Their stories are quite different. One—the Madonna and baby Jesus—looms high above St. Peter's Square, and the other—a mosaic of Christ—is tucked beneath the basilica's high altar.

The mosaic of the Madonna is relatively new, created in the Vatican Mosaic Studio and placed on the façade of the Apostolic Palace in 1981. The image of Christ is ancient, dating back to the original basilica that stood in the same place as today's St. Peter's. Both are examples of the many hidden treasures found in the Vatican today.

The story behind the Madonna mosaic begins with the assassination attempt on Pope John Paul II on May 13, 1981. Four bullets hit the Pope as he entered the square in his Popemobile, and he was critically injured. A few months later, the Pontiff wanted to pay tribute to the Virgin Mary, who he believed had interceded that day to save his life. So he directed that a mosaic copy be made of a painting in the basilica that depicts the Madonna and child. The mosaic, more than eight feet tall, was placed in a window of the papal residence, overlooking St. Peter's Square.

Each time I saw the mosaic—particularly at night when it glowed under a spotlight—I was reminded of the Pope's homage to the woman he considered his personal savior, a devotion made deeper after nearly losing his life.

The mosaic beneath St. Peter's high altar is a tribute of another sort, reflecting the beginnings of the Catholic Church. It marks the site of the Apostle Peter's grave, which lies directly below the altar in the Clementine Chapel. The eighth-century mosaic depicts Christ holding a Bible.

The first time I saw the mosaic, I had entered the chapel to take some photos. Shafts of light suddenly appeared from a window high above. Surrounded by sarcophagi of former Popes, I turned to see the mosaic of Christ, which seemed to be staring at me, and I knew I was in a sacred place.

—*James L. Stanfield*

The Holy See

In St. Peter's Basilica, a service for the consecration of new bishops brings a red tide of cardinals, about 40 as I counted them one Epiphany. Clad in scarlet, each wearing his red zucchetto, the cardinals informally took their seats just below the high altar.

Television lights came on "just two stops less than full sunlight," as photographer Jim Stanfield measured the brightness. The crowd murmured with excitement. Next came a cloudburst of applause, the rousing Roman greeting for His Holiness Pope John Paul II. His miter bobbing in acknowledgment, the Pope made his ceremonial way to the altar. The crowd cheered; many waved handkerchiefs; one man brandished an African fly whisk.

Thirteen candidates, from places as different as France and the Philippines, were ordained as bishops that January day. Each received his miter, ring, and crosier, the shepherd's staff. Each knelt before the Pope for his laying on of hands. And each became a concelebrant of the Mass with the Pope.

At a special moment in the service all the attending prelates, cardinals and bishops, rose and filed past the kneeling new bishops, each placing his hands upon the newly consecrated heads. The long ceremony had a far longer history: These clerics were continuing and affirming the ancient apostolic succession. Every new bishop can trace his consecration—hands to head, hands to head—in an unbroken, two-millennial line to the Apostles themselves.

The cardinals in attendance that day represented only a fraction of the College of Cardinals. The college, currently numbering more than 160 members, is scattered in dioceses around the world; the cardinals meet, all of them, only when called to Rome on some urgent matter of policy, or to elect the successor to a pope who has died. Only cardinals under the age of 80 are eligible to be papal electors.

Those princes of the church at Epiphany were chiefly members of the

Shepherd of the world's largest communion, Pope John Paul II delivers Easter greetings in 56 languages from the central loggia of St. Peter's Basilica.

Roman Curia, the civil service of the Holy See. If the pope is the head of the church, then the curia is the hand, assisting with all the details of governing this giant communion. Presided over by the Secretariat of State, an office headed by a cardinal who acts as the pope's chief of staff, the curia studies and recommends policy in both political matters and those of faith and morals. It looks after a voluminous correspondence and handles the daily work of international diplomacy, papal trips, research and translation, and staff recruitment. It also tends to investments, bequests, and budgets.

After studying the ways of the curia, scholars have variously described its organizational chart as "the labyrinth" and "ponderously baroque." It includes 9 congregations, 12 pontifical councils, 5 offices, 25 commissions and committees, and 3 tribunals, which act as courts dealing with canon law. The congregations and councils are working committees of cardinals and bishops and their staffs. Although the membership includes prelates from all over the world, it is the cardinals residing in Rome who do most of the work and have the most influence.

The work of the congregations ranges over the world and beyond. Details of liturgy, teaching methods for schools, supplies for missionary hospitals—one or another of the congregations will have expertise and purview.

First among the congregations is the Congregation for the Doctrine of the Faith, known before 1908 as the Sacred Inquisition, and colloquially called the Holy Office. It hews to the straight and narrow of belief, policing the theology taught in Catholic institutions and by Catholic theologians. It warns, reprimands, and silences those whom it finds guilty of offending the faith or Christian morals.

Perhaps the most famous case to come before the old Inquisition was that of Galileo in 1633. The mathematician and astronomer supported the Copernican theory that the earth revolves around the sun. The geocentric clergy were shocked. Galileo was forced to abjure the Copernican doctrine, and the court of the Inquisition issued this verdict: "We say, sentence, and declare that you, Galileo . . . have rendered yourself . . . vehemently suspected of heresy: namely, of having believed . . . the doctrine, false and contrary to sacred and divine Scripture, that the Sun is the center of the world. . . ."

The Inquisition condemned Galileo to prison for life, though Pope Urban VIII commuted the sentence to permanent house arrest. Later, the scholar was

PRECEDING PAGES: Statues of saints overlook St. Peter's Square, filled with Easter Sunday worshipers. John Paul II stands on the basilica's loggia in the far distance.

famously quoted as having muttered, "*Eppur si muove*—nevertheless, it moves."

Though some dissident Catholic theologians may feel otherwise, another Galileo affair is unthinkable. If the Congregation for the Doctrine of the Faith seems mysterious, well, it deals with religious mysteries. And it has never claimed to foster secular due process. Certainly, no one is now jailed. And in this post-Copernican world, the Vatican even supports the study of astronomy with an observatory and scholars of international fame—a scientific project entirely supported by the Holy See. No more Galileos.

At the influential Congregation for Bishops, I asked Archbishop Justin Rigali just how many bishops were now in the service of the church. "About 4,200, including those of both the Western and Eastern rites," he replied. New bishops are consecrated each year; others die. The Congregation for Bishops advises the pope on appointments in most of Latin America, Canada, Europe, and Australia, as well as in the United States, except for the diocese of Fairbanks, Alaska, which is a mission diocese and thus under another congregation. Since each bishop outside Italy is required to visit the Vatican at least once every five years, there are many letters to write and arrangements to make. To keep in touch, Archbishop Rigali's office has just 27 employees.

Even the powerful Secretariat of State has a surprisingly small staff. Physically as well as administratively, the secretariat is close to the pope, just down a majestic hallway, frescoed with 16th-century maps, from the papal apartment. "You hear people talk about our 'vast bureaucracy,' " says Monsignor James Harvey, a veteran of eight years in the secretariat, "but in the general affairs section we have only 90 priests and 12 sisters—they mostly do secretarial work—and the diplomatic section has a staff of 30."

The Holy See also supports a diplomatic service in 123 countries. Almost all the diplomats are trained at the Pontifical Ecclesiastical Academy, the alma mater of a number of popes. "They have as good a diplomatic corps as any in the world," a U.S. Foreign Service officer told me.

Another organization speaking for the Holy See with a global voice is

Vatican Radio, managed by Jesuits. To reach people in countries without access to clergy or to free information, the studios schedule newscasts, interviews, music of all kinds, papal homilies, and Masses. Powerful shortwave transmitters broadcast messages worldwide in 34 languages.

Because it accepts no advertising, the radio is a major contributor to a serious cash-flow problem confronting the Holy See. The situation was illustrated for me when I visited Alfons Cardinal Stickler, former head of the Vatican's archives and library. When I dialed his residence, he answered the phone himself. "I have no secretary," he explained. A retired curial cardinal would likely receive less than $3,000 a month; a secretary would easily take half that. When I knocked at the cardinal's door a bit later, he himself let me in. "No porter, either," he smiled.

Cardinal Stickler had recently turned 80, the retirement age established by Paul VI. A distinguished scholar, he had lately moved into an apartment just outside the walls. He was wearing a plain black cassock, a prince of the church quite without pomp: short, rosy-faced, and peppery.

The cardinal's parlor was a big room with a high ceiling. It had one window and was furnished with heavy chairs from the Vatican warehouse and large religious paintings. The effect was one of institutional sterility, a big waiting room.

Cardinal Stickler looked around and laughed. "Yes, in other times cardinals came from wealthy families, or they were given fortunes later. They had palaces with throne rooms. But now there is no money."

*H*is Eminence has a point, though ledgers can be confusing. The Vatican has three separate administrations: one for the diocese of Rome, another for the State of Vatican City, and a third for the Holy See. The diocese is on reasonably sound footing, thanks to an Italian government subsidy. And the city-state, after providing municipal services, still makes a modest profit from museum entrance fees, from the sale of postage stamps, and from shops selling postcards and books.

The Holy See, in administering the affairs of the worldwide church, has only two sources of income: interest from a modest investment portfolio and donations to an annual collection-plate appeal. That once-a-year collection, made in every

Catholic church on or near the feast of Saints Peter and Paul in June, is called Peter's Pence. And since roughly one-third of the pence comes from U.S. Catholics, the fall of the U.S. dollar in the late 1980s reduced that income. In addition, the Vatican bank, somewhat ethereally called the Institute for Works of Religion, was caught up in the tangled investments of Italy's Banco Ambrosiano and had to pay out millions for losses when Ambrosiano collapsed in 1982.

In 1987, the Vatican opened its financial ledgers to the public for the first time. *Fortune* magazine examined the books, and had this to say: "With investments of some $500 million, the Vatican commands fewer financial resources than many U.S. universities."

Naturally, the church has assets in real estate and art, which do not bear interest income. And individual dioceses have money quite independent of the Vatican. Orders such as the Dominicans and Jesuits have separate funds. "But their money doesn't belong to us," one prelate says a bit wistfully.

The curial bureaucracy has grown as a result of an ecumenical council, the Second Vatican Council, opened by John XXIII in 1962. Such a council—a gathering of all the bishops of the church—has supreme authority over the church in matters of faith, morals, worship, and discipline. In the last four centuries there has been only one other council.

The council summoned by Pope John lasted more than three years, largely into the reign of Paul VI, and brought big changes in the church. The Latin Mass gave way to the language of each country. Bishops were given more responsibilities. And a more open atmosphere infused relations with other denominations and religions.

Even saints-to-be face revised rules. At the offices of the Congregation for the Causes of the Saints, Monsignor Robert Sarno gave me a briefing on the work of his office, in a building just outside St. Peter's Square.

"Now the procedure of canonization has three levels," said Monsignor Sarno. "First, gathering of proof—that's now done by the local diocese. Then the study of materials, and finally the judgment process."

A miracle "granted by God through the intercession of the candidate" is necessary before a person is beatified, that is, given the title "blessed" and certified by the church as worthy of local honor. (Someone who dies for the faith as a martyr, however, does not need a miracle to be beatified.) After beatification, another miracle is needed before sainthood. To confirm the existence of a miraculous medical cure, the churchmen ask the opinions of doctors. If the cure is instantaneous, lasting, and scientifically inexplicable—and the evidence is strong that it took place through the candidate's intercession—the churchmen will present the case to the Holy Father to judge whether a miracle has occurred.

Saints can be expensive, though far less so than myth avows. Kenneth L. Woodward, in his book *Making Saints*, notes that "Vatican officials would sooner talk about sex than money." And therewith, he himself estimates the recent cost of canonizing Mother Elizabeth Bayley Seton, the only native-born American saint, at more than $250,000.

The most recently proclaimed saint had been Marie Marguerite d'Youville, whose canonization I had witnessed. Beatified in 1959, she had remained a candidate for sainthood more than 30 years. Her cause was championed by a French priest, Father Constá Bouchaud.

The process was thorough. Dr. Jacalyn Duffin, a hematologist and now a professor at Queens University in Ontario, was asked to read 14 bone marrow specimens taken from a single patient. "They gave me no details at all," she told me. "For that reason, I assumed it was for a lawsuit."

The bone marrow came from a woman who had suffered from acute myeloblastic leukemia. Dr. Duffin, who is not herself a Roman Catholic, was called to testify before an ecclesiastical tribunal. "There was just no medical explanation for the patient's prolonged second remission."

Father Bouchaud had not been sure that the panel would accept this leukemia case. "So I had another miracle in my other hand!" he told me. His second cure was a young boy who had suffered an abnormality that completely vanished.

Father Bouchaud carefully protects the privacy of the miraculously cured patients. "But you saw them both at the canonization. They gave presents to His Holiness at the high altar." I tried to recall the individuals in that long service, but my memory—fogged, perhaps, by incense—was also protecting their privacy.

Honoring Christ's example, the Pope washes the feet of 12 priests on Holy Thursday at St. John Lateran.
FOLLOWING PAGES: In St. Peter's Square, flowers from the Netherlands frame the Pope on Easter Sunday.

Diplomacy looms large on the agenda of the world's smallest nation, a state of affairs fostered by the globe-trotting Pope John Paul II—and his deep concern for world peace. In his library (below), the Pontiff greets fellow countryman Lech Walesa during the Polish President's state visit. Credited with smoothing relations with Eastern Europe, retired Secretary of State Agostino Casaroli (opposite) strolls through Raphael's Loggia between his successor, Angelo Cardinal Sodano, at right, and Bishop Francesco Marchisano.

With a conductor's deftness, Master of Liturgical Ceremonies Monsignor Piero Marini (opposite) orchestrates arrangements for Palm Sunday, one of hundreds of sacred events he oversees each year. Even more duties fall to his eminent companion, Bishop Dino Monduzzi, Prefect of the Pontifical Household. The bishop's purview includes trips, audiences, and special papal events. At right, Alfons Cardinal Stickler, retired head of the Vatican Library, takes a moment to fix his rosary during a pause in Easter services.

FOLLOWING PAGES: At dawn, a full moon sets over St. Peter's Square, where larger-than-life-size figures take part in the Vatican's Nativity scene.

*C*lutching a symbol of her faith, a woman watches devoutly as John Paul II appears at his window before Christmas to bless worshipers and their religious objects destined for home devotions.

FOLLOWING PAGES: Mellow light and a haze of incense suffuse St. Peter's Basilica as the Pope blesses the Nativity scene.

A basilica and the beliefs it represents find their focus in the papal altar, far beneath Michelangelo's dome and the bronze canopy of Bernini's baldachino. With chalice raised, Pope John Paul II (below) celebrates Mass for the ordination of bishops.

FOLLOWING PAGES: Bird's-eye view lends scale to the vastness of St. Peter's, as the new bishops prostrate themselves before John Paul II. Such ancient rites belie the modern complexities of far-flung dioceses. The challenge in the church today is to foster unity, while allowing local bishops the freedom to adapt liturgy and law to a wide variety of cultures.

Faces etched by worldly trials fill with hope in St. Peter's. Opposite, an Italian farmer awaits the Pope during an audience. Wheelchairs ring the papal altar (below) at the Our Lady of Lourdes Mass for the sick and handicapped.

FOLLOWING PAGES: Candlelight ceremony concludes the Our Lady of Lourdes Mass, during which each participant receives Pope John Paul's personal greeting.

Fingertips of the faithful polish Christ's knees, barely within reach of a diminutive pilgrim, on a bronze door inside the basilica. Prayer finds varied expression among the millions of Christians who visit the Vatican. Shadows magnify the gesture of one suppliant, kneeling at a barricade before the Pope's window.

In the steps of countless worshipers before her, a nun (opposite) kisses the bronze foot of St. Peter, first bishop of Rome. Traditionally attributed to 13th-century sculptor Arnolfo di Cambio, the statue rests on a Renaissance marble chair atop an 18th-century jasper pedestal in the basilica. Below, a spray of orchids embellishes the folds of St. Peter's gown. The extended foot has been worn smooth through ages of veneration.

*P*ersonal style of a vigorous Pontiff enlarges the traditional blessing delivered at Wednesday audiences in St. Peter's Square—or, since its 1971 completion, in the Paul VI Audience Hall, where Swiss Guards watch over as many as 9,000 visitors.

"*Long Live the Pope!*"
*Interlocking V's, shorthand
for "Viva," spell a rousing
Italian welcome from
schoolchildren expectantly
awaiting a papal audience.*

*FOLLOWING PAGES:
Outstretched arms of his
admiring compatriots greet
the former Karol Cardinal
Wojtyla, the first non-
Italian pope since 1523,
during a special Christmas
audience for Poles in the
Paul VI Audience Hall.*

Rambo, a black cat adopted by the Vatican Swiss Guard, opens the door to the soldiers' kitchen while I take his photo. The sequence, clockwise from upper left, still makes me chuckle as I recall the cat and his antics.

Vatican Surprises

WHEN PEOPLE HEAR THE WORD "VATICAN," most think of the Pope, the head-quarters of the Catholic Church, the pomp and ceremony surrounding the Church, or maybe the incredible collection of treasures housed there.

Yet I discovered another side to this holy place, a side rarely seen: an every-day world filled with regular people living in the midst of a remarkable setting. The human side to the Vatican is not immediately visible—and it reveals itself in unexpected moments that inform, entertain, and sometimes surprise.

Looking back, some examples come to mind: A modest Polish couple ner-vously taking their wedding vows in a Vatican parish church, surrounded by the grandeur of the city-state; children of the Swiss Guard celebrating birthdays in their Vatican homes with balloons and cake; altar boys playing soccer with all the exuberance you'd expect from youngsters anywhere; Vatican firefighters in alien-looking uniforms poised by the Pope's helicopter in case a fire should erupt.

But without a doubt, the most amusing episode I witnessed during my lengthy stay in the city-state involved the Swiss Guard kitchen and a black cat named Rambo.

"Watch this, Mr. Jim," said one of the nuns who worked in the kitchen early one morning. "I bet you've never seen this before." With that, she disappeared through the passageway from the nuns' quarters to the soldiers' kitchen and closed the glass door. I looked down, and there stood Rambo. As if on cue, the cat jumped up from the ground, grabbed the door handle, and—with a twist of his hip—gave the handle a bounce, turning it to the right. To my surprise, the door opened, and the black cat sauntered into the kitchen, staring back at me as if to say, "Did you get that?" The nuns broke out laughing when they saw my expression.

I soon learned that the Swiss Guard had adopted Rambo, teaching him tricks, and the feline had the run of their quarters. To this day, I laugh out loud when I recall the image of that black cat making his way into the kitchen, look-ing for his next meal.

Behind-the-scenes stories like this kept reminding me I was among regu-lar people doing their jobs and fitting in fun whenever possible. These stories helped create a complete picture of life inside the walled enclave of the Vatican.

—*James L. Stanfield*

As the Pope prepares to board his helicopter, Vatican firefighters stand at the ready in case of a fire.
Their unusual uniforms caught my eye, reminding me of the Tin Man from The Wizard of Oz.

An altar boy, off duty from altar responsibilities, uses a bee smoker to calm bees before opening the hive to gather honey. I found the youngster's protective clothing particularly photo-worthy.

Swiss Guards, who are charged with protecting the Pope and his properties, practice a customized blend of karate and judo developed especially for them. That day, I was struck by their monochromatic outfits, which were in stark contrast to the colorful uniforms for which they are most known.

The City-State

The State of Vatican City has no aimless, uninvited wanderers. You can sign up for an escorted tour of the gardens. You can buy a ticket for the museums and see wonders such as the Sistine Chapel—all under the watchful chaperonage of guards and guides.

But stroll in the gates and just walk about? Don't consider it. A gaudy Swiss Guard politely salutes and directs you to an office of the *Vigilanza*, the working police force. You and the Vatican must have mutual business.

"An appointment with whom, sir?" There's a form to fill out, a confirming phone call, and the officer writes you a pass. Then you enter one of the two main gateways through the Vatican walls; they are as different as city and suburb.

The Arco delle Campane, Arch of the Bells, on the southeast side, leads into the Square of the First Christian Martyrs. A spot in the center of the square marks the original site of Emperor Caligula's obelisk; somewhere nearby, St. Peter is said to have been crucified. Beside a patch of greenery rises the Teutonic College, a pilgrims' hostel in early Christian days and now a residence for German priests. Except for the curbside gasoline station (three pumps), the Vatican through this entrance has the feel of a university campus. A perpendicular campus: Behind St. Peter's dome, a landscaped hill rises 245 feet.

To the northeast, at Porta Sant'Anna, a traffic light on Italian soil mitigates the congestion of cars; you enter the city-state and are instantly downtown. On your right stands St. Anne's Parish Church, nuns bobbing in and out, and on your left, the Swiss Guard barracks. Ahead on the right is the main post office.

"Our postal service dates from the 14th century with apostolic couriers," notes Father Angelo Cordischi, inspector of the Post Office and Telegraph. He is a priest of the Don Orione Fathers, though most of his 65 helpers are lay people. They handle some 4 million outbound letters and 15 million postcards annually.

Outstretched thumb and fingers symbolizing the Trinity, a new Swiss Guard swears allegiance to the Pope. The annual investiture takes place on May 6—the anniversary of the 1527 sack of Rome.

Father Cordischi's staff was sorting envelopes; pigeonholes were marked for various offices; one said "Holy Father." Vatican stamps, prized by collectors, were first issued by the papal state in 1852. Today, the stamps are printed in both Switzerland and Italy.

A shelf in the sorting room held a large trophy. "That's our Vatican Cup," said Father Cordischi. "Our soccer team won it this year. We have teams from the museum, the Vigilanza, technical services . . . and yes, the Swiss Guards—they're young and run fast, but not the best." The mail is clearly faster.

Nearby, on narrow Pilgrim Way, are the buildings of *L'Osservatore Romano, The Roman Observer*, the quasi-official newspaper. A noisy printshop was turning out the news ("The Pope's Week," "The Holy Spirit, Source of Church Unity," read headlines). Some 15 old Linotype machines were gradually being retired; 8 stood at parade rest, while others clankingly set molten type.

L'Osservatore Romano is published daily in Italian, weekly in five other languages, and monthly in Polish. Advertising? "Oh, the Italian edition takes all kinds of ads—for cars, everything. We don't," said Monsignor John Muthig, then editor of the English edition. Problems? "Plenty," he laughed. "The Holy Father quoted St. Thomas Aquinas not long ago, and we made a mistake in the translation. Part of our job is to keep the Pope infallible."

Computers are taking over the printing. The high-tech rooms seem strange inside the Vatican, but change is nothing new. The Polyglot Press—so named for the 30 or so languages of its books—uses a building that in other centuries served as a stable and a foundry for casting bronze statues.

Across the street, trucks deliver supplies to the back door of the supermarket, known as the Annona. To enter one must have better credentials—or a face more honest—than mine. It's sometimes easier to enter the Pope's private apartments (which I did) than to go into the supermarket (which I couldn't). There's a reason: The Vatican must guard against black marketeers. Food, tobacco, and alcohol are cheaper here than in stores outside the walls, and Italian shopkeepers have protested the competition. One museum employee lost his Annona shopping rights when officials learned that he was trading cheap butter to a restaurant for meals.

The city-state is, of course, a company town. And the city manager is a Roman nobleman, Marchese Giulio Sacchetti. He is tall, perhaps six-four, and has

PRECEDING PAGES: Sunday demonstrations in St. Peter's Square sometimes express disagreement with Vatican policies. Here, Italian Jews rally in support of recognition for the State of Israel.

steel-gray hair and a courtly deference. His father, Marchese Giovanni Battista Sacchetti, was a member of the old Papal Court dissolved by Paul VI in 1968.

The marchese administers streets and gardens, as well as the postal service, the fire department, the pharmacy, and sundry other services. He maintains all buildings, office space, and extraterritorial properties, including Castel Gandolfo, the pope's rural summer residence. "And of course, the museums, the tourist information center, and the police. But not the Swiss Guards—only their quarters. The city-state has a good budget. We make a contribution to the Holy See."

*T*he Vatican city-state has 1,200 employees working inside the walls; its extraterritorial employees number more than a thousand. A quasi-union represents the lay workers. Once there was even a near-strike. "Not a real strike," says the marchese. "The museum employees merely refused to work on a holiday."

The marchese's office window offers a generous view: the cumulous bulk of St. Peter's dome, along with magnolias, palms, and a hillside where small plants outline the papal coat of arms. This example of horticultural skill is the work of Elio Cortellessa, chief technician of the Vatican gardens, and his staff of 30.

The Cortellessa family lives in an attractive villa within the walls. The 10-year-old daughter, Arianna, goes to a Roman school, but Antonio, 13, serves as an altar boy, so he attends the altar boys' school just off Piazza Santa Marta, next to the basilica. That means getting up and over to St. Peter's early.

I followed Antonio and 41 other boys to work one wet winter morning. The sacristy was all hush and hurry. Shoes squeaked on marble floors and the boys—a gangly, long-legged bunch between 11 and 14—crawled out of raincoats and into red cassocks and white surplices. A bare light bulb illuminated the carved Latin command overhead: SILENTIUM. We obeyed.

Directing the traffic was Father Mario Laurenti, a native of Malta and once an altar boy here himself. During a brief lull, he explained: "This time of year, we have about 60 Masses a day in St. Peter's. At Easter we'll have 130. But each boy has no more than two a day." While the priest spoke, one lad poked another in the back, grinned, and tried on a fast face of innocence.

"They play and shout and disobey like all normal boys," said Father Laurenti. "But this is their work. They come mostly from the north of Italy. The Vatican pays half the cost of their schooling and board; their parents pay the rest." Altar boys, though Vatican residents, are not normally among the roughly 400 citizens of the city-state. Only permanent employees and their spouses and children are granted such status.

*S*wiss Guards become citizens for their term of service in the Vatican. Volunteers must be veterans of the Swiss Army and between 19 and 30 years old when they sign up for a 2-year tour of duty. They must also be Catholic, "of good family," and unmarried. Charged with protecting the pope and his properties, the Swiss Guards make up the sole remaining unit of the papacy's former army. Their service dates from 1506, when Pope Julius II, impressed by the caliber of Swiss soldiers, arranged with several Swiss cantons to send recruits.

Swiss Guards are irresistible to photographers. And to young women in Rome. "Merely the uniforms," says Corporal Stefan Meier, a bit shyly. But what uniforms! Multicolored, paneled like perpendicular Venetian blinds, jaunty and dashing. But was the designer really Michelangelo? No. The present uniform was worn first in 1914, designed by a commander of the guards.

Living in the barracks was no problem for Stefan Meier at first. "Then, seven years ago, I met Caroline here in Rome," he says with a sigh. Caroline is also Swiss, and blonde and petite. Very pretty. "We cannot marry until I can have an apartment in the Vatican. I like the Swiss Guards, but I wish. . . . " Only eleven such apartments are available to Swiss Guards; officers, even unmarried ones, have first call on them. Fortunately, waiting was worth it for Stefan. Some weeks later, with a 100-watt grin, he announced that an apartment inside the Vatican would soon be available, and "we'll be married in September."

Living inside the Vatican is quiet. Unsurprisingly, religious services cadence the daily routine. The Swiss Guards have their own chapel, as do the altar boys, the hospital, and the convents. The Teutonic College and the Ethiopian College have complete churches; the Ethiopian Church of St. Stephen—the oldest in

Vatican City—dates from the fifth century. (Today home to a handful of seminarians, the Ethiopian College was originally given by Pope Sixtus IV as a hospice for Ethiopian pilgrims.) The pope has a chapel in his apartments.

The gardens, the curving driveways, the harmony of architecture and terrain—all give this 108.7-acre enclave a surprising sense of ease and spaciousness. But some people recall that the atmosphere has not always been so serene. During World War II, when Hitler occupied Rome, Vatican City was crowded and tense.

"Refugees were everywhere," notes Father Robert Graham. He is the Jesuit who has edited the papers of the wartime Pontiff, Pius XII. A white-haired, wiry man, Father Graham is as full of learning as of years. "In the Vatican itself, there were German deserters, Jews, Poles conscripted by the Germans, Italian dissenters. Remember, too, the Vatican made room for the diplomats from countries at war with Italy.

"Half of Rome was clandestine then. You assumed that all papers were false. And ration tickets. Feeding the refugees was touch and go. Mother Pasqualina Lehnert, the papal housekeeper, passed out pasta from the Pope's own supply.

"And, of course, the Vatican was great for espionage. The British ambassador, Sir D'Arcy Osborne, was getting escaped prisoners of war into safe refuges. For this he needed money, so he ran a black market. Rich Italians would bring Italian currency into the Vatican, and the ambassador would give them credit in the Bank of England. . . . But you should talk to people who lived here then."

So Father Graham takes me to the apartment of Dr. Eva-Maria Jung-Inglessis, "remarkable person, splendid scholar, German." That and more. She is a stately and charming woman with merry eyes.

"Yes, I came from Berlin," she smiles. "I was a student in Geneva when I was denounced by the Nazis for anti-Nazi associations." She was ordered back to Berlin and interrogated, but escaped from Germany by getting a job as a housemaid for a German diplomat in Rome. When the German embassy found her out and tried to arrest her, she ran away again, and eventually found refuge in the Vatican. "Monsignor Herrmann Maria Stoeckle, rector of the Teutonic College, got permission for me to work as a kitchen maid." Dr. Jung-Inglessis pauses. "I washed dishes, peeled potatoes, sorted lentils. I slept in a tiny room next to the laundry.

"I kept my bag packed beside the bed in case the Germans should enter the Vatican. At the college alone there must have been 50 or more people hidden—anti-fascists, Jews, everyone using the wrong name. They slept in the library, in the museum, in the closets. Some people slept in the museum's sarcophagi." Swiss Guards armed with traditional halberds patrolled the city-state's borders; the German troops would never have dared cross over without an order from Hitler.

"Then, in June of 1944—the weather was hot—through a keyhole in the gate, I saw the Germans marching north out of Rome," Dr. Jung-Inglessis continued. "Heads down, a defeated army. The Allies arrived from the south, and for the first time in nine months we ran out into St. Peter's Square and embraced the soldiers for joy! Crowds streamed into the square and called for the Pope, who appeared on the loggia. He thanked God and all the saints for saving Rome."

Dr. Jung-Inglessis lives in one of the wonderfully civilized Roman neighborhoods near the Vatican walls, where Vatican life spills over. For 14 centuries the people in this sprawling area, still called the Borgo, have catered to pilgrims and visitors with food, shelter, and souvenirs. These precincts have survived fire, siege, and even urban renewal.

Near Porta Sant'Anna, church bells mix with the basso growl of tour buses navigating around cars randomly, Romanly parked. Two blocks farther on, barricades bar motorcars, and Borgo Pio becomes a strolling street, untidy, yeasty with life. Clotheslines unfurl laundry from apartment windows. Youngsters play soccer on the cobbles and—when a motor scooter interrupts their game—shout words they shouldn't know. Old men claim benches, smoke, and deplore the world. Housewives gossip. Shops offer fruit, paint, pasta, and rosaries cheaper than in St. Peter's Square. Here Vatican people run their errands.

Restaurants put good food on the table and bad art on the wall. Seminarians and Swiss Guards can tell you where the bargains are. Within a few days, the visitor notices familiar faces; people nod in recognition. The Gypsy beggarwoman even gives up wheedling. The visitor has become a regular in the Borgo, part of the Vatican's own eternal village.

Rifle at the unready, a Swiss Guard recruit struggles with a bolt on his first day of firearm training.
Guards soon become proficient with guns, but keep them in the barracks for emergency use only.

Haphazard performance marks the second day of drill for novice halberdiers. Swords and traditional halberds—part pike, part battle-ax, mounted on six-foot handles—are the weapons Swiss Guards carry smartly on patrol. These days they also carry cans of Mace-like spray, and since the attempted assassination of the Pope in 1981, they have studied karate and judo with a black-belt master. At full complement, the Guards number a hundred.

110

*T*rombones and French
horns blaring, the Swiss
Guard band rehearses for
the May 6 swearing-in
ceremony. Their practice
ground is the heliport
landing pad in a distant
corner of the Vatican.
Beyond the pad rises St.
John's Tower, which Pope
John XXIII used as a
tranquil retreat far from
the heart of Vatican City;
a section of fortified wall
abuts the tower. In the
ninth century, after
repeated plunderings by
barbarians, Pope Leo IV
encircled the Vatican with
the turreted Leonine Wall.
A wall, some of it original,
still encloses the Vatican.

Everblooming tribute to Pope John Paul II, his floral coat of arms adorns the Vatican gardens. Borders and symbols are planted anew each season, so that they remain in flower year-round. Formal gardens, with grottoes, fountains, and pavilions, cover about a third of Vatican City. In their midst, a gardener (right) tends vegetables that supply the Pope's table. Dairy products come from a farm at Castel Gandolfo, the Pope's summer residence.

"*For the glory of Christ and the salvation of souls,*" *Vatican Radio was established in 1931 to broadcast the Pope's words to the world. It still does, in 34 languages, via a 175-ton rotating antenna. Largest of its kind, the antenna stands several miles north of Rome. Along with papal speeches and blessings, Vatican Radio transmits messages, sometimes in code, to church officials abroad; its programs range from newscasts to jazz. The Vatican post office (below) also provides fast, efficient communication. About a thousand letters arrive each day for the Holy Father. Special mailbags (right) direct them to his attention. Collectors and tourists prize the Vatican's stamp issues.*

*A*ngling to "put a little English" on the ball, a robed youngster lines up his shot in a room above St. Peter's sacristy. He and his companions attend the school for Vatican altar boys. Students enroll in the three-year course at age 11; some will stay on and prepare for the priesthood. For two hours before school, the boys are on call to help priests at Mass. Meantime they relax, trading soccer cards and taking turns at the pinball machine.

119

In St. Peter's sacristy, altar boys prepare for Mass by donning cassocks and *surplices (opposite) and by readying chalices for Communion (below).* FOLLOWING PAGES: *Just married at St. Anne's Parish Church in Vatican* *City, a Polish bride signs the register.*

Whether celebrating his birthday or watching his children splash in the patio pool, this married Swiss Guard officer enjoys the pleasures of family life— right below the Pope's rooms in the Apostolic Palace. The guards and their families are among the Vatican's citizens.

FOLLOWING PAGES:
Nuns and other tourists shop for religious souvenirs just outside Vatican walls.

*E*arly fog shrouds St. Peter's Basilica, where a cleanup crew wields brooms and dustpans. Carriage horses in the piazza munch fodder before their first tourist passengers arrive. In the morning quiet, the Vatican prepares for another busy day.

*C*hristmas Eve Mass brings a flurry of activity to St. Peter's. Gardeners decorate the high altar, and one of the sampietrini (men of St. Peter's) shoulders a prie-dieu. Skilled workers, the sampietrini have formed a traditional hereditary corps here for four centuries.

Nuns run the ecclesiastical households of the Vatican, acting as housekeepers, cooks, and telephone operators. These sisters work at St. Pius X Preseminary—the altar boys' school. Here, they lay out lunch, with wine and mineral water, and perform sewing chores. Pope John Paul II brought his household nuns—and their Polish cooking—with him from Kraków.

*M*other Teresa of Calcutta's Missionaries of Charity offer food for body and soul in their Vatican hospice, which opens onto a Roman street. Below, nuns in white saris help a woman into a medieval chapel next to the missionary soup kitchen, where workers feed Rome's homeless (right).

PIVS·XI
PONT·MAX·
AN·III

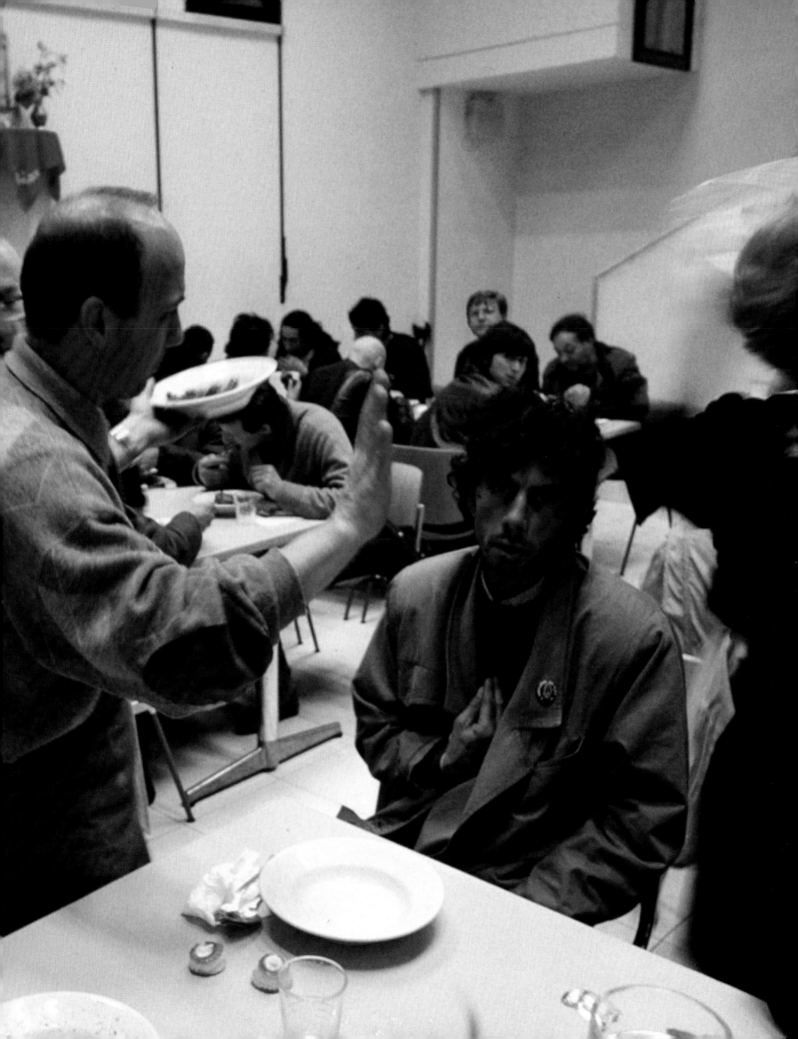

Shoes cast aside, Mother Teresa's missionary nuns kneel at prayer in their private chapel. Pope John Paul II had the hospice built in 1989 at Mother Teresa's request; in addition to supplying hundreds of evening meals, it offers beds to 72 women.

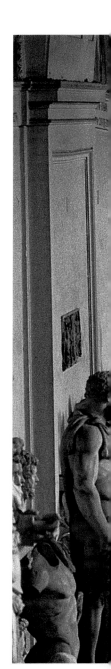

Revenue from art sales is important to Vatican coffers. In the Mosaic Studio, an artist duplicates a mosaic of the Virgin Mary, using the world's largest supply of tesserae in some 20,000 hues. Since the 18th century, the studio has also been reponsible for restoring the vast array of mosaics in St. Peter's. Photographing the many sculptures in the Chiaramonti Museum for a catalog is a daunting task. A German team (below) has been at it for several years.

*S*isters of the Franciscan Missionaries of Mary choose thread from a stock of 6,000 colors to restore tapestries in the Vatican workshop. The famous collection of tapestries needs constant attention. Deft fingers (opposite) repair a masterpiece designed by Raphael, in which Christ gives St. Peter the keys of the kingdom of heaven.

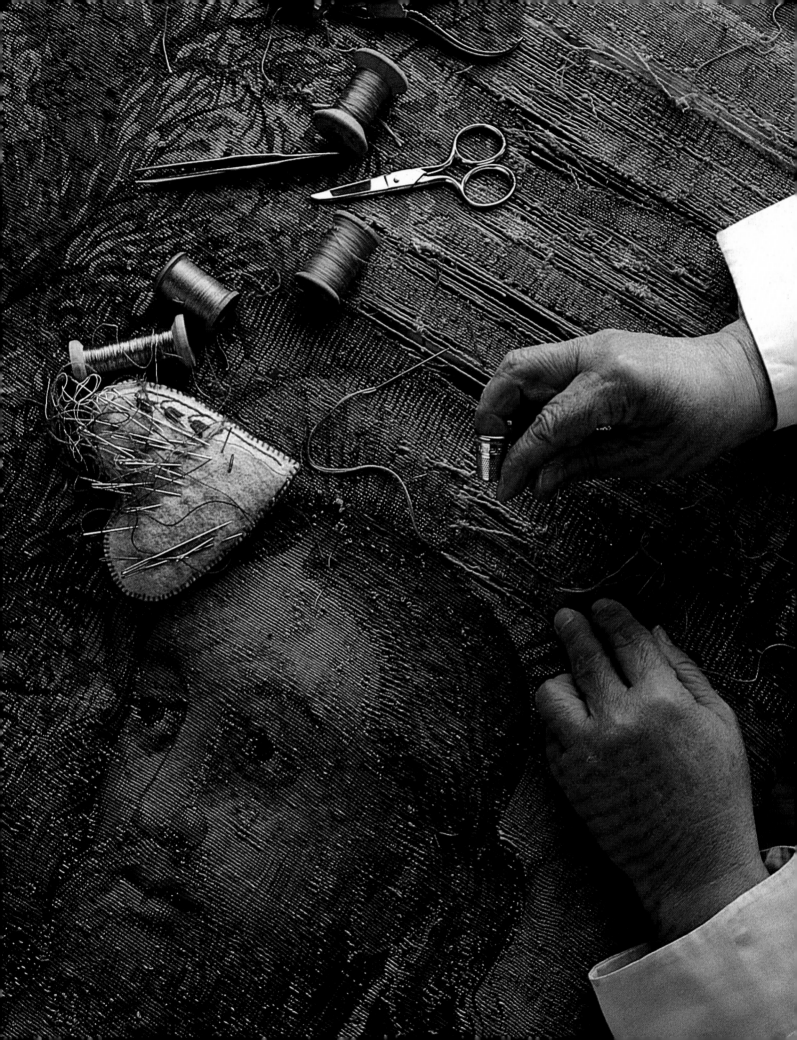

A Vatican altar boy collides with a goal net during a soccer game. During my fieldwork, I spent a lot of time with these youngsters because they made excellent photo subjects and were easily accessible. Typical boys, they were always ready to have fun, even in the midst of their solemn duties.

course of my fieldwork and got a glimpse into their world away from home and family.

The boys ranged in age from 11 to 18. At the time, there were about 40 of them. Most were from northern Italy, but some occasionally came from elsewhere in Europe. While I was there, one boy was from the United States; this was rare, but he was a big help to me, serving as my translator.

I'd often get together with the kids at 5 a.m., when their day began in St. Peter's. For a couple of hours before school, the bleary-eyed boys would gather in a room above the sacristy, on call to help as needed. Between altar assignments, they studied, napped, and played pinball.

Early one morning in the basilica's sacristy, I noticed a few boys huddled together, their crimson robes billowing at their feet. "What's happening?" I asked. One boy whipped a pack of soccer cards out of his vestment pocket. He and his buddies had been trading cards while handling their altar chores.

Their exuberance added an element of fun to the often somber Vatican atmosphere. I covered the boys competing on their school's soccer team against kids from other schools in Rome. I went to their school plays at the Vatican preseminary and watched them perform for their parents. I also saw them fulfill their altar tasks with a reverence that belied their tender age.

Many photographers who cover the Vatican often focus on the Pope. I delighted in finding the hidden gems of everyday life in the city-state. And the altar boys, without a doubt, were one of these gems.   —*James L. Stanfield*

A fully vested altar boy proudly shows off his collection of soccer cards to me early one morning in St. Peter's sacristy. It turned out the boys had been trading cards while waiting for the next service to begin.

A teacher at St. Pius X Preseminary practices a musical number with one of the altar boys. The students were putting on a show for their parents that afternoon, and I was trying to find a visual before the play began when I came upon this intimate scene.

Students from the Vatican's preseminary mingle on stage amid a curtain of colorful streamers. The boys were performing for their parents and teachers, and I got a kick out of watching them act and sing. Between numbers, they seemed to be going in all directions—some kibitzing with friends, others looking backstage, and some nervously staring at the audience.

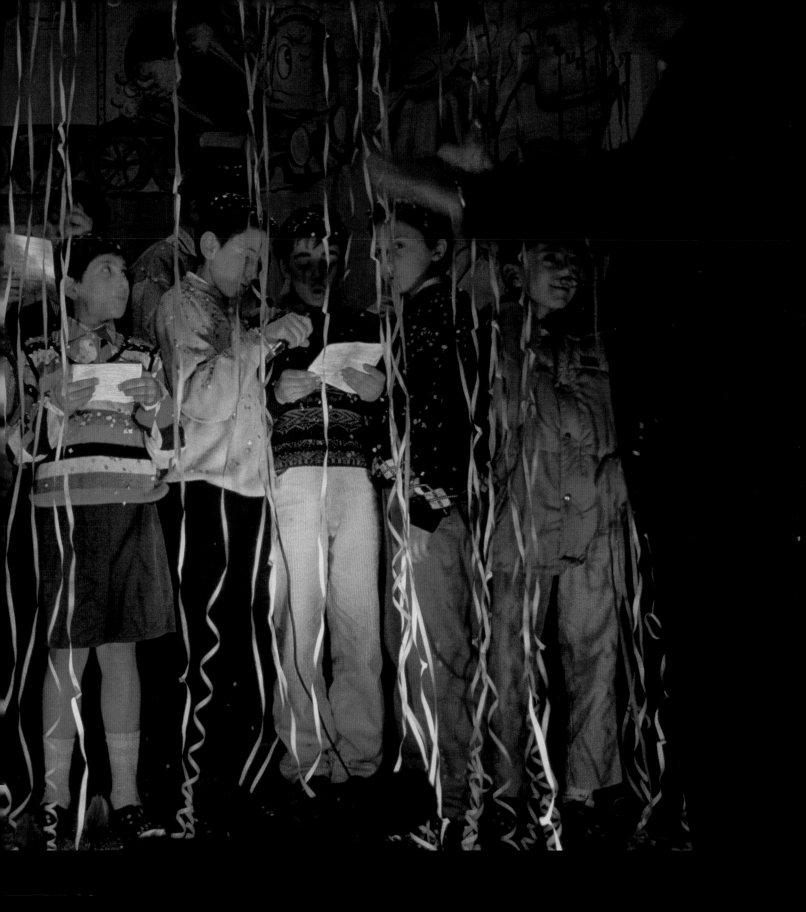

The Treasures

er first visit to the Sistine Chapel was almost ruined for Sally Carter, of Falls Church, Virginia. "It was a hot summer in Rome in 1957," she recalls, "and the chapel was filled with tour groups. The guides were all shouting to make themselves heard. The noise was deafening."

After a few minutes, though, she noticed a Franciscan friar. "He had a guidebook and was completely quiet. He would read a few lines and then look up at the ceiling. He was so calm that the room seemed quiet. So I followed him. When the friar stopped, so did I. When he read his guidebook, I read, too. It was like being alone in the Sistine Chapel, and I saw all of it that way."

Since the day Michelangelo first showed his ceiling in 1512 and "all Rome ... crowded to see it," as a contemporary reported, hordes of visitors have filled the Sistine Chapel. Here Renaissance artists have quarreled, fervent cardinals have elected popes, and hostile armies have encamped. Yet this miraculously decorated place is no stranger to Franciscan calm. It was a Franciscan, Pope Sixtus IV, who had the chapel built and gave it his name.

Today, signs requesting no talking keep the Sistine Chapel relatively quiet, but it is still among the most visited sights in Rome; as many as 20,000 people file through it in a single day. The whole room—some 132 by 44 feet and taller than it is wide—remains the most famous single jewel in the Vatican collections. The art, books, artifacts, and documents that make up the collections are displayed throughout Vatican chapels, galleries, and hallways, and in 14 museums, the Secret Archives, and the Vatican Library.

Many scholars call the 15th-century humanist Pope Nicholas V the true founder of the Vatican Library. He loved manuscripts and collected hundreds of them, some dating from medieval times. When Nicholas died in 1455, an inventory listed some 1,200 manuscripts, 800 in Latin, 400 in Greek. Sixtus IV made it

Sorrowful yet serene, Mary grieves for her Son in Michelangelo's "Pietà." Impeccably restored after a madman's attack in 1972, it remains the best known of the treasures in St. Peter's.

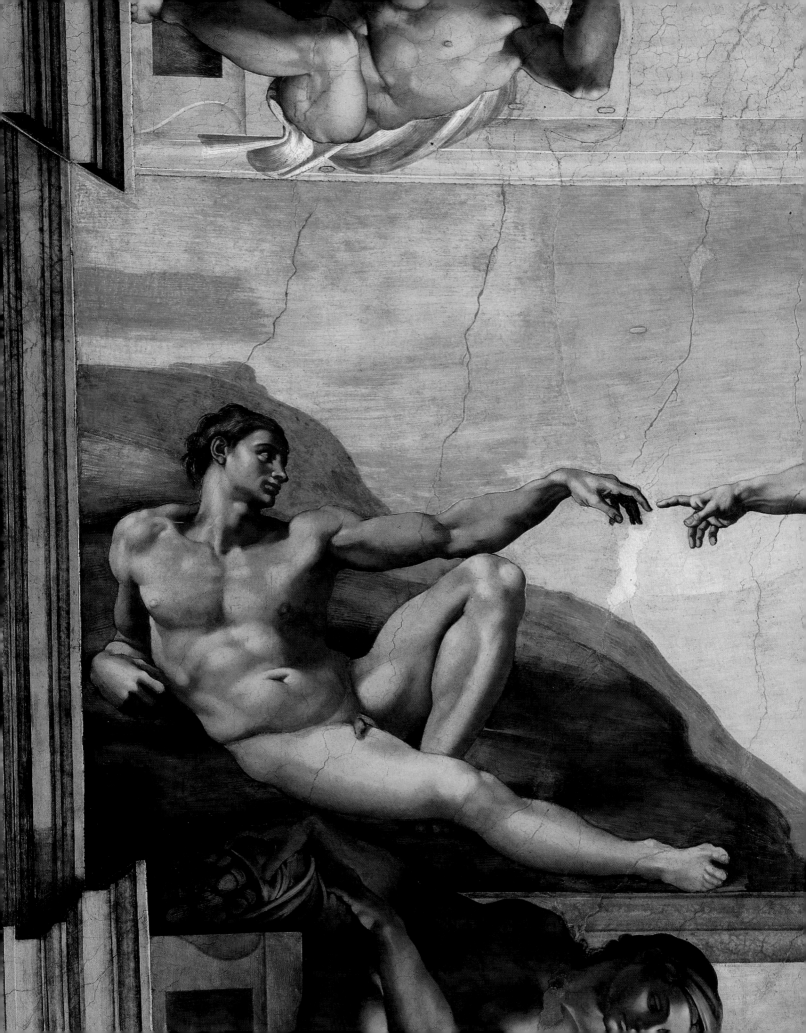

easier for administrators; in 1475 he issued a papal bull that formally established a library structure, made rooms available for the manuscripts and scrolls, and named a librarian. Later popes would separate and define the work of the librarians, archivists, and curators of the museum collections.

The Vatican Library is one of the world's greatest repositories of medieval and Renaissance manuscripts and incunabula, books printed before 1501. "The Vatican was the world's intellectual switchboard at that time," notes Dr. Declan Murphy, of the U.S. Library of Congress. "It was the first institution to put knowledge at the service of government."

Fifteenth-century sketches of now vanished Roman ruins, early maps and music manuscripts, even Greek and Roman coins and whimsical medieval caricatures can all be found in the collection. And scholars are permitted to handle the rare books in a well-lighted reading room. "We want people to feel welcome here," explains Father Leonard Boyle, the library's director. He was once a reader here himself.

Pope Paul V founded the Vatican Archives in 1612. Though their primary purpose is as a repository for the popes' records and files, scholars are admitted by special permission for "this decanting of history," as one cleric has called it. Here is an abdication document of Queen Christina of Sweden, signed by her lords in 1654 and authenticated by 306 seals. A letter written in 1587 by Mary Queen of Scots says, "Today I have had a message . . . that I must prepare myself to receive death." And a love letter sent in 1527 by Henry VIII to Anne Boleyn proclaims, "Henceforward my heart shall be dedicated to you alone. . . ."

The full and proper name for the institution is the Vatican Secret Archives. But names can mislead. " 'Secret' originally meant 'private,' " notes Monsignor Charles Burns. "Like the word 'secretary,' it refers to privacy rather than something confidential." So the archives contain the popes' private files, now open to scholars for all years up to the 1920s.

Likewise the Gregorian Profane Museum. "Profane" simply means "not concerned with religion." So the museum, founded by Gregory XVI in 1844, contains nonreligious art—works from the age of imperial Rome, classical Greek pieces (both originals and copies), and pagan cult sculptures.

Other art collections within the Vatican run the gamut from Egyptian to

PRECEDING PAGES: Imparting life with a touch of His hand, Michelangelo's God completes the Creation of Adam, one of nine Sistine Chapel ceiling frescoes depicting events from the Book of Genesis.

Missionary-Ethnological (all of its pieces come from non-European countries) to Modern Religious; the latter, housed in the former Borgia Apartments, includes 550 works in the bouquet colors of Matisse and the stained-glass brilliance of Rouault, and even works by avowed communists like Picasso and Diego Rivera.

The growth of the Vatican's classical art collection began in 1503, when Julius II, on becoming Pope, brought a marble statue of Apollo from his own palace and placed it in the Belvedere Courtyard, now part of the Pio-Clementine Museum. Of course, this Greek god appealed to old Julius, the warrior grandson of a fisherman; Apollo was "he who strikes from afar," an avenger. Irascible, syphilitic, and coarse, Julius had lived the life of a soldier, but as a nephew of Pope Sixtus IV, he had sharpened his eye for art.

Through the centuries, the "Apollo Belvedere" has continued to affirm Julius's taste. As the great 18th-century German classicist Johann Joachim Winckelmann wrote, "Of all the works of antiquity that have escaped destruction, the statue of Apollo represents the highest ideal of art."

Three years after Julius placed the "Apollo Belvedere" in the Vatican, another remarkable statue was found on Rome's Esquiline Hill. Scholars recognized it from a description written by Pliny the Elder; the piece had stood in the palace of the Emperor Titus. It shows Laocoön, a priest of Apollo who had warned fellow Trojans about the wooden horse, and his two sons being punished by the goddess Athena; the three struggle hopelessly against two monster serpents. Pope Julius couldn't resist: Soon after the discovery of the "Laocoön" group, the Pope bought it for the Vatican.

Pope Julius II could pick artists as easily as statues. After he saw a sculpture by a young Florentine still in his twenties—the "Pietà" by Michelangelo Buonarroti—the Pope set him to work, and kept him working even when money ran out. "I have not received any money from the Pope for thirteen months," Michelangelo once wrote his father. ". . . I am penniless. As a result I cannot be robbed."

Julius had come to the papacy only a few weeks after the death of his enemy, the Borgia Pope Alexander VI. The Borgia Apartments, luxuriously frescoed by such artists as Pinturicchio, made Julius uncomfortable. He complained that the rooms carried a "foul and villainous memory." So he moved to new quarters. On the advice of his architect, Donato Bramante of Urbino, Julius brought a young artist, also of Urbino, to paint his new suite. He was the brilliant Raphael Sanzio, eight years younger than Michelangelo. Their rivalry soon became intense.

As a contemporary biographer explained, "Bramante and other rivals of Michelangelo put it into the Pope's head that he should have Michelangelo paint the vault of the chapel of Pope Sixtus IV." If the sculptor should refuse the fresco project, he could alienate the Pope; if he accepted the offer, his inexperienced work with a paintbrush would be unflatteringly compared to the murals of Raphael.

Later Michelangelo wrote, "All the dissensions between Pope Julius and me arose from the envy of Bramante and Raphael. . . . They wanted to ruin me; and Raphael had a good reason . . . for all he had of art, he had from me."

Paint the ceiling? "It is not my trade!" insisted Michelangelo. He was proud to be a sculptor. But Pope Julius was adamant. And even as the sculptor painted in wet plaster, he continued to grumble in written verse to the Pope: "My Lord. . . . I am thy drudge. . . . the more I toil, the less I move thy ruth."

But on his scaffold, the sculptor-now-painter worked arduously: standing, arm raised, painting straight up over his head. Again in verse he wrote: "My beard points to heaven . . . and my brush, continuously dripping onto my face, turns it into a rich mosaic. My loins have penetrated my belly, my rump's a counterweight. . . . and I am stretched like a Syrian bow."

He must have been a bedraggled sight. Never handsome—a badly broken nose made his face seem mashed—Michelangelo was also personally untidy. He slept in his paint-spattered work clothes and removed his boots so rarely, one friend reported, that when he did take them off, "the skin came away like a snake's." Unsurprisingly, he had few friends.

"He didn't like anyone," says Gianluigi Colalucci, chief of the Sistine restoration. "Anyone who could take on such a difficult task would have had to be very sure of himself. He had a sense of perfection. Physical strength. Willpower."

Perhaps no other living person has such a deep understanding of Michelangelo as Dr. Colalucci. With his three assistants, he has spent more time on Sistine scaffolds than the original artist. Cleaning away nearly five centuries of candle soot, the restorers came to know both the art and the artist in a singular way.

"We could see how much work he did in one day," says Dr. Colalucci. "His brush strokes are like his signature—done like a sculptor. And his sculpture is like architecture. All his skills are one." And when Dr. Colalucci began cleaning "The Fall and Expulsion from Paradise," he sensed a change. "He starts to enjoy what he is doing. His designs become less constricted."

During his years on the Sistine ceiling, Dr. Colalucci spent his spare time in Padua, restoring some frescoes by Titian. "They were done in the same period as the Sistine Chapel," he says. "But the artists were such opposites. Titian was a pure painter and Venetian. As he paints flesh tones, he leaves a fleck of blue from his brush. He paints the spontaneous Venetian way. Michelangelo is Florentine. Orderly. Never a color where it shouldn't be."

Knowing the two men as he does, which one would Dr. Colalucci prefer as a dinner partner? He doesn't hesitate: "Titian! Michelangelo ate little and badly. But Titian . . . Look at his picture! Titian enjoyed food."

The main challenge in cleaning the Sistine ceiling, Dr. Colalucci says, was to obtain a uniform result. "We had three, then four men working over a nine-year period. We had to clean without showing the personality of each restorer."

The restorers used a long-tested solvent called AB 57, a mixture of bicarbonates of sodium and ammonium with a fungicide, an antibacterial agent, and carboxymethylcellulose. Applied by brush, the cleaning solvent was usually allowed to sit three minutes before being wiped off, along with softened glue and grime, with a sponge soaked in distilled water. The process could be repeated after 24 hours. Every step of the work was monitored.

Before their work was completed in December 1989, the restorers invited a few friends to a party on the scaffold. During the festivities Dr. Colalucci undertook one small bit of cleaning: the space between the nearly touching fingers of Adam and God. To the applause of guests, he cleaned that last barrier between the human and the divine. "And we hoped the scaffold would not fall."

Now, in the darkened chapel, a custodian throws a switch. "The lights take five minutes to warm up," he explains. We wait. The lights flash and flicker teasingly, off and on, quick bursts of the colors Michelangelo used to re-create all creation. At last, there's an even glow: The world, its history, and its creatures breathe with life.

"Art historians will have to rewrite their books," notes Dr. Walter Persegati, the retired secretary and treasurer of the Vatican Museums. "Michelangelo was unknown as a colorist. A myth had grown up that he veiled everything in darkness for metaphysical reasons—to show the darkness of the ages before Christ. We've destroyed that myth."

Works by other Renaissance masters—Perugino, Ghirlandaio, Rosselli, Botticelli—decorate the walls below the ceiling, but the capstone of the chapel is the painting done for the altar, Michelangelo's "Last Judgment," a theme suggested by Pope Clement VII on his deathbed. The custodian notes, "The painting is pessimistic. Clement remembered the Sack of Rome, and the mood is there. Michelangelo admired Dante and has used figures from *The Divine Comedy.*"

Trying to identify people in Renaissance paintings has become a kind of parlor game for scholars. In keeping with the style of the times, faces of popes and patrons can be seen throughout the Vatican collections. Michelangelo himself appears in a Raphael painting, wearing his inevitable boots.

Michelangelo's young rival had all of the papal apartments to fill. Now called the Raphael Stanze, these rooms show the prodigious output of Raphael and his assistants. Art historians still debate which figures the master painted and which his pupils executed. Amazingly, Raphael spent only 12 years in Rome and during that time had other work to do. He made cartoons for tapestries, wrote apostolic briefs, designed sets for the theater, and oversaw antiquities in the Vatican. When Bramante died in 1514, Raphael was appointed papal architect.

But time was running out. In 1520, Raphael caught a fever, and on April 6—Good Friday and his 37th birthday—the young master died. His masterpiece, "The Transfiguration of Christ," was still incomplete, but the figure of Christ between Moses and Elijah had been done by Raphael's hand. With its otherworldly lighting, "The Transfiguration" became his own visual elegy. The painting was placed beside his body as it lay in state.

On a recent Good Friday, in the Vatican art gallery, a young man from

Guanajuato, Mexico, Raúl Espinosa Nava, studied "The Transfiguration." "In Mexico," he said, "we believe that some people become very good before they die. Maybe Raphael was getting ready to go."

Michelangelo outlived his rival Raphael by 44 years. Art historians would notice that he had moved beyond the classicism of the High Renaissance into the stylized work of the mannerists. At age 75, he painted his last picture, "The Crucifixion of St. Peter," for the Pauline Chapel. Since, as Vasari noted, "using the hammer kept his body healthy," Michelangelo continued to work in stone. But again, as he wrote, "against my will, Pope Paul forced me . . . to work in the construction of St. Peter's." He succeeded rivals Bramante and Raphael as the architect. (He even restored some altered plans to Bramante's original concept.) But he refused any payment—and he continued to grumble.

He fashioned a scale model of the dome, and one model now on display in the Vatican may be his. The master's work merged with others, so that today little in St. Peter's can be clearly called only Michelangelo's. Workmen had built no higher than the drum of the dome when, just short of his 90th year, Michelangelo died. He had worked for nine popes and had outlived the Italian Renaissance.

By the turn of the 17th century, styles of art had grown more dramatic. The age of the baroque had dawned. The term "baroque" may derive from the word that the Portuguese used to describe irregular pearls. Applied to art and architecture, the term came to mean something larger than life, dramatically embellished. To enter St. Peter's Square is to feel a baroque embrace. The colonnade is the achievement of a Pope and a sculptor.

The Pope was Urban VIII, Maffeo Barberini, who chose his papal name because he so loved Rome, the city (*urbs*) he was determined to beautify. Urban was a cultivated man who loved music, wrote florid poems, and had the taste—and the revenue—to engage the sculptor Gian Lorenzo Bernini. Together, they glorified the papacy with one of the world's most dramatic settings.

"The bus had picked us up at the airport, and they first drove us *here*," says a young American seminarian of his first view of St. Peter's. His hands sweep 180 degrees, encompassing the 284 giant columns. "Right then I said a prayer."

Bernini himself said many a prayer as his work took form. Intensely religious, he attended Mass every day. Like Michelangelo and like his own stern father before him, Bernini began as a precocious sculptor. As a boy, he went to Rome, where his father was employed by Pope Paul V. There, as his biographer reported, the boy "spent three continuous years from dawn until the sounding of the Ave Maria" studying and copying classical and Hellenistic works and the paintings of Raphael and Michelangelo.

At about age 11, Bernini carved a portrait bust that caught the eye of Pope Paul. The Pontiff entrusted the boy's education to Cardinal Barberini—the future Pope Urban—who was urged to give the boy "fire and enthusiasm."

As Pope, Urban gave Bernini much more. In 1624, he commissioned the young sculptor to fashion a large canopy, or baldachino, over the high altar of St. Peter's, a fitting crown for the Apostle's grave. Bernini conceived this architectural work as a mammoth piece of sculpture, a bronze construction taller than any Renaissance palace still standing in Rome. Yet Bernini wanted this baldachino to convey a feeling of heavenly lightness, even to resemble a portable cloth canopy like those carried over Near Eastern potentates. The columns would have twisted, spiraling contours, for tradition had it that Solomon's temple had been supported by such columns.

The work took nine years—and all the bronze that could be found. Some of the metal came from as far away as Venice; some was even stripped from the portico of the Pantheon and the sides of St. Peter's cupola. When the baldachino was unveiled in 1633, Bernini was acknowledged as an architect of genius.

Later generations found Bernini's style overdone, the gestures too broad, the ornamentation too heavy. "Baroque" became, for a while, a derisive term. But those who feel uncomfortable with the style might take a look at Bernini's last work of art: the monument to Pope Alexander VII in the transept of St. Peter's Basilica. There the old man, nearly 80, expressed his own concept of prayer. He gave it pomp, splendor—and powerful sincerity.

Each day, after the Vatican Museums close, visitors still crowd St. Peter's. Some sightseers head for the overlook that rings the interior of the cupola. The perspective baffles. Mosaic portraits of Apostles loom close, great, and grainy with tiles, while below on the basilica's floor, human figures are shrunk by distance.

Hardy folk climb on up a steep, narrow staircase between the two shells of the dome; construction details are visible here, the work of some 600 laborers and the architects Giacomo della Porta and Domenico Fontana, who inherited the project from Michelangelo. (They finished the cupola in a 22-month fury of work, using torchlight by night, on orders of the impatient Sixtus V.)

Then the climbers emerge for a windy, dizzying view from the panoramic terrace at the base of the dome's lantern; it offers a living relief map of Vatican City, the serpentine Tiber, hilly Rome, and the horizon of Apennines. Viewed from above, Bernini's colonnade and the entranceway to the basilica form the shape of a keyhole, an architectural complement to Simon Peter's keys.

But greater than the spacious spectacle from the top of the dome is the view of St. Peter's inside. At moments of high ritual, the pageantry and the crowds of faithful hide details. In quieter times, with reflective moments to stroll and wonder, a visitor can make discoveries. The flames of votive candles tremble; shafts of sunlight creep along the floor. Penitents study the signs outside a dozen confessionals to find a priest who speaks their mother tongue. Unhurried visitors come and go, examining Bernini masterpieces and relics from Constantine's Old St. Peter's, exploring the grottoes and the many graves of popes, testing rusty Latin on countless inscriptions.

Of all the spots inside St. Peter's Basilica, the one that attracts the largest crowds is the chapel far to the right and near the entrance. Protected by glass and attentive guards, lighted softly, stands Michelangelo's famous "Pietà," the grieving Virgin Mary holding her dead Son. Visitors speak softly if at all and gaze in respect. Some kneel. As one cleric has said, "The 'Pietà' is as much an aid to worship as a work of art."

The Italian word *pietà* means "pity"—but the statue enlarges the word. It shows the overwhelming sadness of a mother who must bury the child she bore. But Mary's face is too young—that was an objection when the young Michelangelo first showed his work. His reason was theological: Mary's purity is the reason for her unlined face. We can even pardon the young artist's touch of hubris. When he heard the statue attributed to another sculptor, Michelangelo took his chisel and carved his name on the ribbon crossing the Virgin's shoulder. He signed no other statue.

In 1964, at the behest of Pope Paul VI, the "Pietà" crossed the Atlantic and was displayed at the World's Fair in New York. Crowds in the New World marveled at it.

The public clamor bore a price. Eight years later, in St. Peter's, a deranged man leapt from the crowd shouting, "I am Jesus Christ!" and frenziedly took a hammer to the work of art. Before he was overpowered, he had smashed away the Virgin's arm and mutilated her face.

Within days, though, restorers were at work. Dr. Nazzareno Gabrielli, now head of the museum science laboratories, recalls the problems. Wearing his white laboratory jacket, surrounded by test tubes and beakers and the scents of a hospital, he discusses the "Pietà" as a physician would his patient. "From October to Christmas, we worked right in the basilica—turning the chapel into a laboratory."

Everyone agreed that since the "Pietà" was an object of veneration, it should be restored, if possible, to look as it had originally. But what if the new materials should discolor in coming centuries? Anything added to the "Pietà" should be something that later restorers could remove without damage. "We had to make many experiments. We found that a polyester resin worked well if mixed with powdered marble," Dr. Gabrielli notes. The scientists were fortunate. "In the 1930s a plaster cast had been made of the original statue. It was not perfect, but it was close. And with this copy, we were able to work like a dentist making teeth. We made a rubber copy of the broken statue, and thus duplicated missing parts.

"We made at least 20 attempts on the damaged eye, trying to get the right color, shape, and translucency. Then we applied the new piece to the statue with reversible adhesive. If the color should change in the future, the piece could be removed and a new restoration method studied."

Is the "Pietà" as good as new? It looks it. But now when visitors contemplate the "Pietà," they can think not only about the grieving mother and her crucified Son, and about the artistry of the genius sculptor, but also about the respectful ingenuity of modern scientists.

Childhood takes winsome form in the "Putto Graziani," a second-century B.C. bronze from the Vatican's Gregorian Etruscan Museum. An inscription identifies the statuette as an offering to Tec and Sans, divine protectors of children.

Hand outstretched to clasp his missing dish, the nearly life-size "Mars of Todi" seems to beckon to visitors in the Gregorian Etruscan Museum. The chance discovery of this late fifth-century B.C. bronze in 1835 drew excited followers, including Pope Gregory XVI, to the new field of Etruscology, and helped lead to the museum's founding two years later. Further impetus came in 1836, when another excavation within the papal domain yielded rich finds from the seventh-century B.C. Regolini-Galassi tomb— among them, a pair of ornate gold arm bands. Attention to detail takes a different shape in a sixth-century B.C. amphora by the Greek artist Exekias. Large numbers of the widely admired Greek vases were uncovered in Etruscan burial sites. Such imports form an important part of the museum's collection.

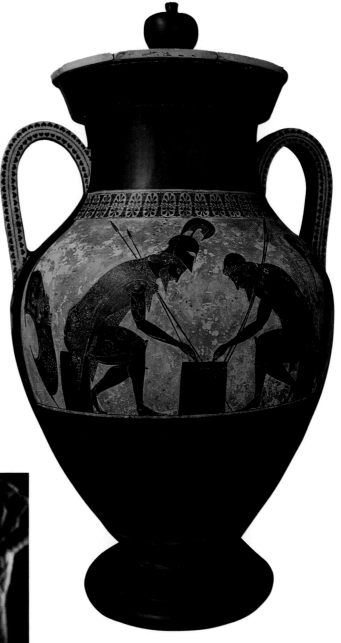

*S*tatuary sculptured in Rome but inspired by Egypt fills Room III of the Gregorian Egyptian Museum. The room is a partial reconstruction of the Serapeum that Roman Emperor Hadrian had built at his Tivoli villa as a tribute to the cult of the god Serapis and to Egyptian civilization. Seeking to broaden contemporary interest in Egyptology, Pope Gregory XVI opened one of the first Western museums of its kind in 1839.

Eloquent fragment of a first-century B.C. statue by Apollonius, the "Belvedere Torso" portrays the Greek ideal of human beauty. The work inspired some of Michelangelo's Sistine Chapel figures—and his belief that its creator was "wiser than Nature." Though the torso is now installed in the Pio-Clementine Museum, its name recalls the sculpture courtyard where Pope Clement VII had it placed in the 16th century.

Condemned by Athena for warning fellow Trojans about the Greeks' wooden horse, Laocoön, along with his sons, writhes in the deadly grip of giant serpents. Famed in Roman times, the group was rediscovered near the Colosseum in 1506. A delighted Pope Julius II installed the work in the Vatican's new Belvedere sculpture garden. There, it joined the "Apollo Belvedere," another of the Pontiff's favorites. The placement of the "Apollo" in the Belvedere Courtyard in 1503 marked the start of the Vatican's acquisition of its extraordinary classical sculpture collection, much of it now in the Pio-Clementine Museum.

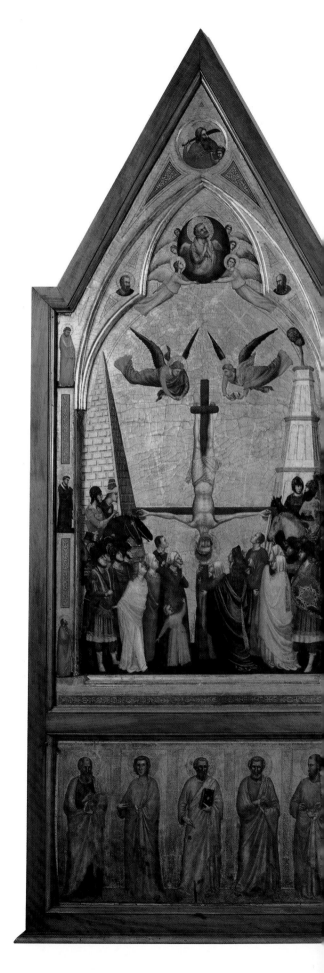

*C*hrist reigns over medieval works in the Pinacoteca, the Vatican's gallery of paintings and tapestries. The oldest, a multitiered "Last Judgment" from the 11th or 12th century, ranks among the finest Italian primitives. In the 14th century, Giotto and his workshop introduced the technique of perspective to their New Testament themes in the "Stefaneschi Triptych." Named for the cardinal who commissioned it—shown kneeling at left by the steps of Christ's throne—the work originally crowned Old St. Peter's high altar.

*T*ransported to first-century Jerusalem, fortifications from 15th-century Rome enhance Fra Angelico's portrayal of the martyrdom of St. Stephen. Cycles from the lives of St. Stephen and St. Lawrence, frescoed on the walls of Pope Nicholas V's private chapel between 1447 and 1450, reflect both the friar-painter's genius and the flowering of Renaissance humanism under his papal patron.

*R*enaissance angels make heavenly music in the Pinacoteca. Melozzo da Forlì's choir originally decorated the apse of Rome's Basilica of the Holy Apostles, where the artist completed his "Ascension of Christ" in 1480. When renovations destroyed the fresco as a whole in 1711, the detached fragments of angels joined other works by Melozzo at the Vatican.

Exotic, richly clad bystanders hear "The Disputation of St. Catherine" before the Emperor Maximinus. Sumptuous detail, in art as in life, suited the worldly tastes of Alexander VI, the Borgia Pope who commissioned this and other frescoes by Pinturicchio for his private apartments in 1492.

FOLLOWING PAGES: Freed from the grime of centuries, Michelangelo's fresco of "The Fall and Expulsion from Paradise" glows with renewed vibrance in a section of the Sistine Chapel ceiling. Smaller panels at top and bottom depict other stories from Genesis— "The Sacrifice of Noah" and "The Creation of Eve"— flanked by figures of sibyls and prophets.

*C*hrist appears to His disciples on Mount Tabor in a detail from Raphael's "Transfiguration." The artist was working on this masterpiece of balance and harmony when he died on April 6, 1520—his 37th birthday. Favorite painter of the late Renaissance in Rome, Raphael had turned his talents to other mediums, including sculpture, architecture, and cartoons for a series of tapestries devoted to St. Peter and St. Paul. Commissioned by Pope Leo X for the Sistine Chapel in about 1515, the tapestries, which were woven in Brussels, included the exquisite "Miraculous Draft of Fishes" (below).

Raphael's powers reached their peak in "The School of Athens," one of the frescoes in the Stanza della Segnatura. In 1508, Pope Julius II had commissioned the young artist to decorate it and other rooms in his personal apartments.
In this painting of the great thinkers of antiquity, some bear the features of Raphael's contemporaries. Plato, with white beard and the face of Leonardo da Vinci, stands with Aristotle at center. The model for brooding Heraclitus in the foreground was the artist's rival, Michelangelo, shown wearing the boots he seldom removed. Raphael even included himself, peering from behind the white-clad figure at far right.

FOLLOWING PAGES: Antechamber to the Sistine and Pauline Chapels, the Sala Regia was frescoed in the late 1500s by Giorgio Vasari and other artists. Today, Vatican officials greet visitors here.

176

*I*n his "Martyrdom of St. Erasmus," painted about 1629, French artist Nicholas Poussin employed a restraint that offsets his barbarous subject. His cool, classical style contrasts with the passionate realism of Caravaggio, another 17th-century painter represented in the Pinacoteca. The work of one artist of the same period, Gian Lorenzo Bernini, epitomizes the splendor of the baroque. His bronze "Throne of St. Peter" (opposite), in the apse of the basilica, encloses a medieval wooden chair. A sunburst around a dove representing the Holy Spirit caps the huge masterpiece.

*E*stablished by Pope Paul VI in 1973, the multinational Collection of Modern Religious Art expresses "the religious, the divine, the Christian" through paintings and sculptures donated to the Vatican. British painter Graham Sutherland executed his "Study for the Crucifixion" (above) in 1947. The work Georges Rouault called "Sainte Face," from about 1946, hangs in a room of his art.

*S*phere within gleaming sphere, Arnaldo Pomodoro's 1990 sculpture, "Sfera Con Sfera," stands in the Vatican's Pigna (Pinecone) Courtyard. Casting massive globes or columns in bronze is Pomodoro's specialty. The fractured surface reveals a complex inner structure reflecting the difficulties of the modern world at the end of the second millennium. Paired pastorales, or crosiers, made by artist Lello Scorzelli, have served two popes. Both Paul VI and John Paul II carried the one in the background. On his 70th birthday, May 18, 1990, John Paul II was presented with the crucifix in front, which he now carries as his own.

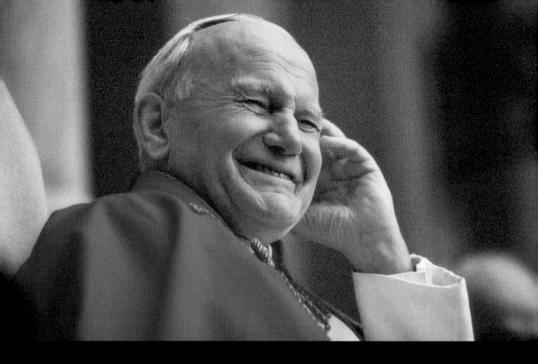

Pope John Paul II laughs during a skit in a Vatican courtyard on Easter Sunday in 1991.
I attended the afternoon performance, which included lots of "flying whipped cream."

After the play, members of the acting troupe lined up to meet the Pope, and a clown greeted the
Holy Father. A Vatican photographer told me John Paul enjoyed comedy—particularly slapstick.

Portraits of a Beloved Pope

SIX MONTHS INTO MY FIELDWORK, I still had a huge gap in my Vatican coverage—I had yet to gain direct access to Pope John Paul II.

For weeks I had been writing letters to the Pope's personal secretary, Monsignor Stanislaw Dziwisz. My goal: to shoot a day in the life of the Holy Father. I wanted to capture ordinary moments in the life of an extraordinary man.

One day, while covering a Vatican birthday party, the daughter of the Pope's private physician and a member of the Swiss Guard encouraged me to write a personal letter to the Holy Father. Both were often in his presence and promised to hand-deliver the letter for me.

I carefully crafted the note, making it clear I didn't want to break his stride or interfere in any way with his commitments. I only wanted to provide informal glimpses of him in a tasteful manner. Along with the letter, I included 15 of my photos depicting life in the Vatican. Then I held my breath. I was scheduled to return to the United States in a matter of days.

Within 36 hours, Monsignor Dziwisz approached me after a private Mass for Czech citizens. I will never forget his words: "The Holy Father and I think your photos are splendid. Please meet us at the helipad at 4 p.m." And before I knew it, I was off to cover the Pope at his summer residence at Castel Gandolfo near Rome.

Suddenly my access to the Holy Father seemed endless: an invitation to a private breakfast with local dignitaries; entry to his private chapel, where he knelt in prayer; access to an Easter Day skit put on for the Pope by lay leaders.

One morning, I received a message: "Be at the Bronze Door at 11:45 a.m." I was invited to the Pope's study for the Angelus, the noon blessing given on Sundays. An assistant showed me into the room, saying I had 30 seconds to make three photos. John Paul walked out of his bedroom, ready to begin the Angelus, and asked me with a friendly smile, "How is the book going?" All I could think was, "I have only 30 seconds!" Fortunately, I was given more time.

These occasions, combined with my coverage of papal audiences, allowed me to create a special selection of portraits—many never before published— that display the warm, deeply holy, and fun-loving nature of this beloved man. My persistence and patience had paid off.

—*James L. Stanfield*

John Paul blesses a girl in St. Peter's Square during an audience with a group of Spanish youths. I watched the youngsters respectfully wait in line for the opportunity to greet the Holy Father.

The Pontiff blesses the crowd as the wind picks up in St. Peter's Square in 1985. I made this photo just as Monsignor Stanislaw Dziwisz, the Pope's personal secretary, reached for the Holy Father's cloak to put it around his shoulders. Cardinal Jacques Martin, Prefect of the Papal Household, stands at the Pope's right.

The Pope prays in the Garden of Our Lady at Castel Gandolfo near Rome. I had been struggling for months to get direct access to the Holy Father, and a personal letter I wrote to him helped open the door. With only a few hours' notice, I was invited to fly in the papal helicopter to the Pope's summer retreat in the Alban Hills.

The Modern Papacy

In the information booth next to St. Peter's Basilica, Sister Lucy, of Our Lady of Sorrows, encounters all sorts of human problems and requests: directions and translations for confused travelers, lost wallets and children, and runaways like a boy named Giuliano. "He came from the city of Taranto in southern Italy, and he arrived one afternoon asking to speak with the Holy Father. His family had some problems, and he felt sure the Pope could help him."

Sister Lucy explained kindly that His Holiness prayed for everyone, including him, and the Pope hoped that boys could stay with their families. She persuaded Giuliano to call home, fed him a meal, and "got permission from my Superior to take the boy to the train station. He asked me to thank the Holy Father."

Like young Giuliano, millions of the faithful regard the Pope with familial trust and affection. And when a pope dies, as one Roman woman said, "We mourn. We feel like sheep without our shepherd." The church has faced this personal loss 263 times. Tradition brings comfort—and a new shepherd.

When a pope dies, the cardinal camerlengo, or dean, summons the College of Cardinals to Rome for a conclave to elect a successor. The Sistine Chapel is made ready, and nearby rooms are converted into dormitories. The papal apartments are locked and sealed. Fifteen to twenty days after the pope's death, the cardinals assemble in the Pauline Chapel for the Mass of the Holy Spirit.

Their Mass complete, the cardinals leave in procession to the music of the hymn "*Veni, Creator Spiritus*—Come, Creator Spirit," passing through the grand audience hall—the Sala Regia—and into the Sistine Chapel. The 120 cardinals eligible to vote are all under the age of 80.

"*Extra omnes!*" the conclave marshal announces. "Everyone out!" Thus the conclave to elect a new pope begins with a locked door, for the very word

Bishop's crosier pressed to his brow, Pope John Paul II prays during Mass in the Vatican's Pauline Chapel.

"conclave" derives from the Latin words for "with" and "key." "Three persons lock the door from the outside," notes Marchese Guilio Sacchetti, the Vatican city manager. "They are the prefect of the pontifical house, the commandant of the Swiss Guards, and the delegate for the State of Vatican City—in this case, myself." The key is then kept by the delegate. "Of course, I have to move a bed into my office so I can stay close by. Some of the cardinals are old men and in poor health." Twice the marchese has served as keeper of the conclave key, each time spending two nights in his office.

Through the centuries, the form of pontifical elections has varied. Temporal rulers—even mobs—have tried to influence the selection; sometimes they have succeeded. But no longer. The isolated cardinals now elect a pope by one of three procedures: by *inspiration* (acclamation), by *compromise* (negotiation), or by *scrutiny* (secret balloting requiring a two-thirds majority). Scrutiny has been by far the most common recent method. In centuries gone by, the deliberations have included not only persuasion, but also threats and even bribery. But always, always prayer. The saying is simple: "Cardinals have elected, but God has chosen."

And when the choice is made, the camerlengo asks the candidate: "Do you accept?" A heavy question that can turn ambition into anguish. Some men must have wanted to refuse. But when a candidate answers, "I accept," in that instant of assent he becomes the successor to the See of St. Peter.

The pope-elect is then escorted to an adjoining room. There he finds white papal cassocks in three sizes. He chooses one, changes from the colorful garb of a cardinal—and spends some moments alone. What is it like, this historic room?

Archbishop John Foley, head of the Vatican's office of communications, fetches a key, and we fumble down the dark hall behind the Sistine altar. The key makes a scraping sound, and we enter a small room of irregular shape, built long ago, perhaps for storage, certainly not for ceremony.

The light is blinding bright, and the overwhelming color is red: Scarlet damask covers a chaise and panels the walls. The room has one small mirror, no pictures at all. Why red? Maybe to match the vestments worn for martyrs . . . maybe even for courage. Or perhaps the color scheme has no scheme at all. But the name of the room says everything: the Room of Tears.

Once the new pontiff is dressed, it is time to burn the ballots and send the

PRECEDING PAGES: Beyond the Vatican's borders, John Paul II presides over Holy Thursday rites at the Basilica of St. John Lateran, his seat as Bishop of Rome.

puffs of white smoke up the chimney—the signal of resolution to the expectant crowds in St. Peter's Square. The camerlengo then appears on a balcony and shouts "*Habemus papam!*—We have a pope!"

Five times Marchese Sacchetti has watched the white smoke rise from the Sistine chimney.

"Every good Roman waits in the square to see the white smoke. I was 13 when Pius XI died in 1939. I can remember seeing the dome of St. Peter's lighted by torches—very romantic and beautiful." The marchese has known each of the popes since Pius XII, except for John Paul I, who reigned only 33 days. "All popes are impressive to me—all of them remarkable."

The Roman Catholic Church counts 264 popes, beginning with St. Peter and his martyred successors. The first 35 popes are all considered saints. The 36th Pope, fourth-century Liberius, an irresolute man who contributed to the squabbles between Rome and Constantinople, has the distinction of being the first uncanonized bishop of Rome.

For more than 400 years "we have had no wicked popes," one priest said. "We have been quite fortunate in our modern popes."

Pius IX served for nearly one-third of the 19th century, the longest pontificate to date. In 1846, he entered the papacy as a reformer, granting amnesty to political prisoners and exiles. But in 1848, revolutionaries laid siege to the Pope's offices and murdered his prime minister. Pius himself escaped disguised as a simple priest. Not until 1850 could he, with the help of French troops, return to Rome. A decade later he saw all the papal lands, except for Rome and its outskirts, annexed into the new Italian kingdom.

In ecclesiastical matters, Pius IX had more success. He oversaw a spiritual renewal in the church, while working to centralize its authority. In 1869, he called together the First Vatican Council and proclaimed the doctrine of papal infallibility, asserting that when a pontiff defines an issue of faith or morals *ex cathedra*, in his role as supreme pastor, he speaks with infallible authority. But Vatican I never completed its work.

In September 1870, Italian forces seized Rome itself, and the papal state was no more. Rome had become the capital of the new Italy. Pius IX and his immediate successors chose never again to set foot outside the Vatican. He died so unpopular in Rome that a mob interrupted his funeral procession and tried to toss his body into the Tiber.

Leo XIII represented a change of style, flexible in politics, open to new ideas. He encouraged the study of sciences, reactivated the Vatican observatory, and opened the Secret Archives to researchers of all creeds. "The church has no secrets," he said sincerely. Scholars consider his most famous manifesto, *Rerum Novarum—Of New Things*, the beginning of modern Catholic social teaching. It endorsed a concept of trade unions, condemning the "inhumanity of employers and unbridled greed of competitors." Leo frightened some reactionaries, but came to be called "the workers' pope." He brought the papacy, literally, into the 20th century before he died in 1903.

*P*ius X was the last Pope to be canonized, a man of "transparent goodness and humility," as one historian has written. He died just as World War I began. His successor, Benedict XV, was an experienced diplomat, a background that served him well during the war. But his peace proposals were hampered by his diplomatic isolation and the Vatican's unresolved political status. Not until 1929 could Pius XI bring "Christ's peace in Christ's kingdom." The Lateran Treaty he negotiated that year with Italy, creating an independent, neutralized Vatican City, finally freed the church of its own temporal worries.

But other temporal concerns crowded in on Pius XII when he came to the papacy in March 1939. As Cardinal Pacelli and secretary of state, the future Pius XII had drafted an encyclical denouncing Nazi beliefs as anti-Christian. He saw his role as the Pope of peace, and he used all his diplomatic skills to prevent the war that began six months after his own pontificate. Later he was criticized for relying too much on traditional diplomacy in the face of Nazi atrocities.

Slender and ascetic, peering with a scholar's eyes through thick spectacles, he seemed "the last of the great aristocrats," recalls Viola Kiesinger Wentzel, the daughter of a former West German chancellor. "But he also had warmth and charm. He spoke German well."

"I remember his hands," notes Paola Brandt Kenneally. "Fingers so long and expressive." Her grandfather was the Secret Chamberlain of Cape and Sword in the papal court, so she used to play in the Vatican gardens as a child.

The first Pope to become widely known through radio and television, Pius XII used the media to promulgate his concern with liturgy; he devoted more than 200 documents to the way of life of religious orders.

In the last years of his pontificate, bad health isolated Pius from the public, so the change in manner and personality seemed great when the warm, outgoing John XXIII came to the papacy. He was short, with a large nose and ears and the girth of a man who loved food. Once he reportedly turned away from a mirror with the words *"come sono brutto*—how ugly I am." He was no such thing: He had a merry smile and a radiant kindness that charmed people of every background.

Born the third of 13 children into a peasant farm family, the future Pope served in World War I as a hospital orderly and later as a chaplain, a splendid preparation for his role as "the people's Pope," as he came to be called. So was his service as a diplomat for the Holy See. As Pope, John had the self-assurance to begin talks with East Europeans and even to receive Nikita Khrushchev's son-in-law. He opened dialogues with Christians of other communions such as Ecumenical Patriarch Athenagoras and Archbishop of Canterbury Geoffrey Fisher. He greeted some Jewish visitors with the words, "I am Joseph, your brother." And he had the inspiration to call the historic Second Vatican Council, which set in motion a means for modernizing and renewing the church.

"My husband worked for him when he was Archbishop Roncalli and stationed in Istanbul," a woman told me recently. "Of course, we had not even met then. That was during World War II." Her future husband was a political refugee from a Nazi-occupied country, and fearing the Germans would occupy Istanbul, Archbishop Roncalli sent him to a sanctuary in Rome. "I was also a refugee living in the Vatican," the woman said, "but we did not meet until after the war. We fell in love. And by then the archbishop had become Pope John. When His Holiness heard that we were to be married, he consented to perform the wedding ceremony. But we had to keep it secret so others would not make the same request.

"So we had no wedding pictures. But afterwards, Pope John gave us a special present, a silver box and inside it—no, not a rosary or a medal, but money for our honeymoon! *That* was Pope John."

Practical, thoughtful, romantic. He visited parish churches on the spur of the moment. And prisons. Romans loved John for his open manner and impulsive visits, and nicknamed him Johnny Walker.

When the serious and hardworking Giovanni Cardinal Montini succeeded Pope John as Paul VI, Romans bestowed another nickname: Dry Montini. But that was a misnomer. Paul's knowledge of curial procedure uniquely qualified him to implement the revolutionary work of Vatican II. True, Pope John had once described Cardinal Montini as "a little like Hamlet." But caution served him well. And beneath his bookish reserve, Paul had a special kindness.

Archbishop Justin Rigali thinks of Paul VI "as a teacher and spiritual father. He showed great compassion when my brother was ill with cancer." Archbishop Rigali has served the last three popes. As he did for Paul VI, he acts as translator for John Paul II when distinguished visitors pay calls. In each pope he has valued "a unique richness." He remembers the last day of the brief pontificate of John Paul I: "He received a group of Filipino bishops, and he told them, 'We must do more to help the poor. At the same time, we must speak to them of heaven!' He was thinking of heaven that last day of his life. A man of great simplicity."

And John Paul II? "Incredible energy! He travels to dozens of countries, and he seems to live on two planes: united with God and also with the problems of man. I've seen him extremely tired after a day of travel; then he goes to his chapel to pray for half an hour or so, and he's completely rejuvenated."

As a figure of history, John Paul II has a special place. A journalist in Rome speculates this way: "He was the catalyst for change in Europe. The Polish Pope made the Solidarity movement possible. And *that* made the thaw in Poland possible. All the rest follows." No wonder someone wanted to kill him.

Wednesday, May 13, 1981, was a balmy, springtime day in Rome. A crowd—more than ten thousand people—had gathered in St. Peter's Square for the weekly papal audience. As the Pope was driven around the square in his open car, people cheered. The car moved slowly; parents held their children up, and John Paul caressed one youngster. Abruptly, the people heard pistol shots. The Pope faltered and fell back, his white clothing bright with blood. In the crowd there were shouts, screams, and a convulsion of movement. Someone—the identity of that bystander is still a mystery—apparently jostled the arm of the gunman.

"I would have continued to fire if someone near me had not shoved me with force," said Mehmet Ali Agça, an escaped Turkish murderer, after he was seized by the angry crowd. As policemen took the man into custody, a way was cleared for a stand-by ambulance rushing the Pope to a hospital two miles north. A moan swept the square as the news was announced over loudspeakers. People knelt on the cobblestones to pray.

Surgeons worked five and a half hours to repair the bullets' damage to the abdominal cavity, right arm, and left hand. The Pope's recovery took months.

The trial and conviction of Agça—and the investigation of a possible Bulgarian conspiracy—took far longer. But after his recovery, John Paul visited the would-be assassin in prison; their conversation has never been revealed.

Whatever the origins of this threat to his life, John Paul continued to keep open his lines of communication with officials in Eastern Europe. And he has continued to move unflinchingly into crowds of people, blessing the crippled and ill, kissing small children, touching the faithful and even the curious.

*P*ublic audiences are lively and long. In fair weather, they are held in St. Peter's Square, the better to accommodate large crowds. But during winter or rain, the site is the Paul VI Audience Hall, a modern auditorium seating 9,000 people. Four resplendent Swiss Guards march out to take their places, parade rest, halberds at the ready. Lights signal the shining moment: His Holiness John Paul II enters from the left. He walks with characteristic, Churchillian stoop, the result of a shoulder injury in his youth. He waves to the applauding crowd, makes the sign of the cross, and takes his seat. By language—French, English, Spanish, Portuguese, Polish, and Italian—visiting groups are introduced. Some rise quietly; choirs sing hymns when their names are called. Others break into full-throated cheers. With a raised hand, the Pope acknowledges each group. He then addresses the crowd, sometimes carrying themes from week to week.

After leading the faithful in the Paternoster, the Holy Father descends the marble stairs and begins greeting people. As he approaches, women smooth their hair and men straighten their neckties. Nuns turn into giggling groupies. Camera lights flash. Some pilgrims give presents to the Pope, others hold up rosaries for his blessing. Then His Holiness moves away and, with a final benediction, he is out the door. It happens every Wednesday.

*H*e is an approachable and magnetic person, this extraordinary Karol Wojtyla, the first Slavic pope. He was born on May 18, 1920, into a modest family in the south of Poland. His father, a retired army officer, brought home a small pension; his mother died when he was a little boy. Karol attended Polish public schools and excelled at his studies—and also at football, canoeing, and swimming. At Jagiellonian University in Kraków he took part in dramatics, wrote poetry, and served as an altar boy. He was assisting the parish priest on September 1, 1939, when the first Nazi planes came. "I served Mass to the sound of bombs and anti-aircraft guns," he later recalled.

He decided to become a priest, and when the Nazi occupation forbade seminaries, he studied in an underground school sponsored by the church. To support himself, he worked as a laborer in a limestone quarry and later in a factory, reading books on theology beside a boiler. He was ordained in 1946, the same year that his first volume of poems was published under the pen name Andrzej Jawien. During the years of Russian occupation, he was sent to Rome and the Pontifical University of St. Thomas Aquinas, known as the Angelicum.

Appointed archbishop of Kraków by Paul VI, he proved himself an astute diplomat in dealing with the Communist government and was named a cardinal in 1967. Vatican II brought him international attention and eventually wide travels. In the conclave of 1978, his fellow cardinals elected him Pope.

"The best mind of any pope in the last 500 years." That's the opinion of a young seminarian studying in Rome. Youthful enthusiasm, perhaps, but no one can prove otherwise. A voracious student of linguistics, John Paul speaks five languages fluently and several others with varying command. (On his worldwide

broadcast each Christmas and Easter, he pronounces a greeting in 56 languages.)
He stays relentlessly busy, rising at 5 a.m. to ready himself for prayers and Mass in
his private chapel. Visitors gather outside in Bernini's colonnade near the famous
bronze doors to the Apostolic Palace; the sounds are few in St. Peter's Square.
The clocks of the basilica strike, and then the bronze doors grind open with a
heavy, basso clunk. Swiss Guards stand in the doorway to welcome the guests and
show them to the chapel in the pontifical apartments.

His Holiness is at prayer when the few invited visitors and clerical concele-
brants join him. The chapel, small and clean-lined in red and white polished marble, seems designed for echoes. But there is no sound at all. The Pontiff prays with
complete concentration. If the Pope's gestures seem theatrical in his audiences or
at the high altar of the basilica, there is no hint of self-consciousness in his private
Mass or in his intense conversations with God.

Every day is full. His personal secretary, Monsignor Stanislaw Dziwisz, keeps
a close watch on his appointments and schedule. And John Paul delegates much of
the day-to-day work of the Holy See to his secretary of state. But between meetings with foreign dignitaries and church officials, the Pope also makes the most of
working meals with his staff. (Until John XXIII, popes traditionally ate alone.)
Polish nuns prepare his food. "The Holy Father eats everything and with relish —
and not just Polish food," says one monsignor who often dines with him. "For
supper he eats lightly — soup, cheese, perhaps fruit, and a glass of Italian wine."

When he can, the Pope takes enthusiastic exercise. There is no swimming
pool in the Vatican, but Castel Gandolfo has one. And when he is in residence at
that country palace, John Paul likes to go for vigorous six-mile walks. After his
crowded Christmas schedule, John Paul sometimes goes skiing in northern Italy.
This square-jawed, active man seems too young to be in his 70s.

He likes to sing. In Poland, he joins in with choirs singing familiar hymns.
When he was serenaded in Mexico, he added his own robust baritone — and Spanish — to the romantic *"Cielito Lindo."* He enjoys broad humor. Photographer Jim
Stanfield took pictures of the Pope watching a skit by a religious group; when
whipped cream covered one plump boy, "the Holy Father broke up laughing."

By habit, John Paul goes to bed early. Seminarians keep track by watching the
windows of his apartments: top floor corner is his bedroom, the next window

is his study. "He's up late—maybe the international situation," they guess.

Traditionally, Tuesday is the pope's day off; no audiences are scheduled then. Paul VI used Tuesdays to write, in Italian, his messages for the Wednesday audience, revising his manuscript until the last minute. John Paul drafts his messages in Polish, leaving ample time for translators to do their work.

Much of the Pope's time is devoted to religious ritual. A special Mass may take two or three hours, and the Pontiff is on television virtually all that time. There's no opportunity to look tired or irritated or to take a moment's rest.

During the seasons of Advent, Christmas, and Epiphany, pilgrims from all over the world come to see the splendor of services in St. Peter's. Holy Week—from Palm Sunday until Easter Sunday, the greatest feast of the Christian year—is a time of almost continuous ritual for the Pontiff.

Between Holy Thursday and Easter Sunday, during a recent Holy Week, I computed that John Paul was on public view for more than 20 hours. In the Basilica of St. John Lateran—"the mother and head of all the churches," where the Pope claims his seat as Bishop of Rome—he has diocesan duties quite aside from his responsibilities for the Holy See. There he performs the ceremony of washing the feet of 12 priests, memorializing the act of Jesus at the Last Supper, when He washed the feet of the 12 disciples.

On Good Friday, John Paul himself hears the confessions of laymen in St. Peter's, a custom he began a few years ago to stress the importance of this sacrament. In the afternoon, he conducts a commemoration service of the Lord's Passion, also in St. Peter's. And he completes the day by making the Stations of the Cross in the Roman Colosseum. This service, initiated in its dramatic setting by Paul VI, would be taxing for a much younger man. For hours the Pontiff carries a large cross from inside the ruined Colosseum through crowds of the candle-bearing faithful and up an adjoining hill, where he speaks to the throng.

Holy Saturday brings the Easter Vigil, again in St. Peter's and again until late at night. Then it is Easter Sunday in the great square. The steps to St. Peter's have been transformed into a garden in bloom. Bernini's colonnade embraces a festive and growing crowd: 250,000 souls before the morning is done—a gathering that spills into the streets for blocks beyond.

And after the recessional, the papal retinue enters the great door of St.

Peter's, and Pope John Paul, whom we've seen at such close range, becomes a small, mitered figure on the balcony. He speaks to our multitude in this Eternal City and to the world beyond, *urbi et orbi*, and gives us his blessing.

The Vatican, of course, is a congregation of buildings, an accretion of history. Popes leave their individual physical legacies in stone and brick, and these souvenirs tell something about the pontificate of the man. We look at the grotto grave of Pius XII, whose body lies closest to the spot where Peter himself was buried, and we recall that Pius dug into the rich history and traditions of the church and brought about the archaeological excavations beneath St. Peter's. We view the contemporary paintings acquired by Paul VI for the Collection of Modern Religious Art, and we remember that Paul also modernized the church by carrying out the work of Vatican II.

John Paul II will have left many a legacy when his pontificate is done. He has already demonstrated on a global scale his concern for the disadvantaged. His 1991 encyclical, *A Hundred Years,* marked the centennial of Leo XIII's *Rerum Novarum.* In it John Paul called on capitalist countries to do more to meet the needs of the poor; he urged that conscience be made part of economic life.

Close to home, this legacy found architectural expression when Mother Teresa of Calcutta asked him for a place within the Vatican walls. John Paul hurled his energies into the construction of a hospice for her Missionaries of Charity. The building, next to the Holy Office, has a door on a Roman street. There are 72 beds for homeless women, but the kitchen feeds hundreds more, both women and men. Nuns in white saris hurry tubs of salad and pasta to waiting street people. The guests are mostly an unlovely lot: the unlucky and unwashed, drunks, whores, drug addicts, life's discards. They leave their plastic bags near the door; the stench from those possessions fills the hall. A photograph of Mother Teresa hangs on the wall with this inscription: "God speaks in the silence of the heart—and we listen."

Here, inside the Vatican, this house speaks in the silence, saying much about Mother Teresa's missionaries and much about the Pope who brought them here . . . and much, too, about the architecture of love itself.

*M*arble likeness of Pope Pius XI, photographed with a fish-eye lens, rests above his tomb in the Vatican Grottoes. With the 1929 Lateran Treaty, in which Vatican statehood was recognized at last, he and Italy patched up old grievances. But when dictator Mussolini tried to curb church freedom and then, in 1938, adopted Hitler's racist policies, relations deteriorated and finally broke. On hearing of Pius XI's death a year later, Mussolini exclaimed, "Thank God the stubborn old man has gone!"

Gilded and jeweled trappings of Pope Pius XII, on display in the Vatican's Liturgical Treasury, attest to the pageantry of the papacy. But traditional pomp and historical circumstance form an uneasy alliance in Francesco Messina's 1964 bronze statue of the World War II Pope, who gestures defensively as if to fend off the horrors of war.

*S*carlet-covered walls surround the vestment of papal white that a new Pope, Pius XII, donned in 1939 in the Room of Tears. When a cardinals' conclave completes its grueling election task in the adjoining Sistine Chapel, the new pontiff retreats to this modest chamber and selects symbolic garb. Preceded by puffs of white smoke and the cry of "Habemus papam!—*We have a pope!*" he then emerges onto the balcony of St. Peter's to greet the cheering crowds. Inevitably, joy and sorrow mingle; the room's name, of uncertain origin, suggests the gravity of the occasion.

The "people's Pope" in life, John XXIII in death inspires a visitor's devotion at his tomb in the Grottoes. His greatest achievement remains the Second Vatican Council, which in 1962 launched a sweeping renewal in the church. Here John and Vatican II are honored by a panel on Luciano Minguzzi's bronze "Door of Good and Evil."

*M*osaics in Rome's Basilica of St. Paul's Outside-the-Walls piece together portraits of John XXIII's successors. Though not blessed with John's common touch, Paul VI (below, left) vigorously carried on the work of Vatican II. His bespectacled successor, John Paul I, sought to combine the progressive and traditional instincts of the two popes whose names he took, but he died only about a month after his 1978 election. Both Paul VI and John Paul I wore the same jeweled miter (opposite).

*C*alm in the eye of an admiring storm, John Paul II, Bishop of Rome, pauses in a Roman church before yet another public appearance. The ceaseless round still exhilarates the extroverted Pontiff, who in his youth briefly considered a stage career. Emerging from the papal palace via private elevator (right), John Paul enters St. Peter's to say Mass on Christmas Day.

*S*tepping into a confessional and out of his usual papal role, *John Paul II takes the part of an ordinary priest to hear pilgrims' confessions on Good Friday. He began doing so in 1979 to stress the sacrament's importance, thus inaugurating an annual Easter rite. The Pope's day starts with Mass at 7 a.m. in his private Apostolic Palace chapel* (opposite), *attended by his staff of Polish nuns, his two secretaries, and a handful of invited guests.*

*T*orchlight guides the papal party along the Via Crucis, or Way of the Cross, through the Colosseum. An athletic John Paul II carries the cross throughout the Good Friday procession, stopping at each of the 14 stations, which denote Christ's suffering and death. Setting enhances symbolism at one of the world's enduring landmarks, where early Christians faced lions for the amusement of Romans.

PRECEDING PAGES:
Confronting Poland's grim
past, Pope John Paul II
tours Majdanek
concentration camp in
1987. His own birthplace,
Wadowice, is only a few
miles from Auschwitz. Not
one to shy from controversy,
this Pope has ably used the
media to dramatize such
symbolic visits in dozens of
countries.

One symbol of hope is
raised to honor another, in
Gdynia during the Pope's
1987 visit to Poland — his
third in eight years. Nine
of every ten Poles profess
Catholicism, most of them
fervently; even under
Communism the church
remained, as in centuries
before, the bastion of
national identity.

World's most famous Pole greets countrymen as a foreign head of state on the 1987 official visit. Though spiritual office accords him this role, John Paul II is, in fact, often viewed as a political liberator by Poles and other Eastern Europeans, and as a crusading churchman around the world.

OVERLEAF: "I pray for the special heritage of Polish Solidarity," Pope John Paul II tells 750,000 worshipers in Gdańsk, the union's birthplace. Throughout his 1987 trip, the Pope's presence lent the spiritual will that would help Poles cast aside Communism in 1989.

Windows on a Pope's world link his private inner sanctum, the Apostolic Palace apartments, to the public realm beyond. While the crowd in St. Peter's Square squints up toward the fourth-floor chambers, his Vietnamese secretary helps Pope John Paul II prepare for his Sunday blessing, the Angelus.

FOLLOWING PAGES: A reflective Pontiff strolls through the Garden of Our Lady at Castel Gandolfo, his summer refuge in the Alban Hills near Rome.

*Pope John Paul II and Cardinal Joseph Ratzinger exchange Christmas greetings in 1990. In 2005,
the cardinal was elected to succeed John Paul after his death. I sensed something special between
the two men and was delighted to rediscover this image more than 20 years later.*

The Two Popes

IN 1990, I WITNESSED A WARM ENCOUNTER between Pope John Paul II and Cardinal Joseph Ratzinger, and captured the moment on film. Little did I know that 15 years later, after John Paul's death, Cardinal Ratzinger would become the next Pope.

The encounter occurred at the annual Christmas Blessing ceremony, a papal audience when the cardinals offer Christmas greetings to the Pontiff. The event begins the Vatican's holiday season, and the city-state and Rome come alive with decorations, festivities, and Nativity scenes of all sizes.

This wasn't the first time I had seen the two men interact. I had noticed that they were often in each other's company, and it seemed as if they shared a special relationship. A Vatican colleague recommended I focus my coverage on Cardinal Ratzinger, as he was the Pope's confidant and right-hand man.

I learned more about their relationship after my coverage. John Paul had in fact called the cardinal to the Vatican from Germany in 1983 to head the Congregation for the Doctrine of the Faith, one of the most important offices of the Roman Curia—the governing body of the Catholic Church. And when Cardinal Ratzinger was due to retire in 2002, the Pope wouldn't let him go.

John Paul died on April 2, 2005, and Cardinal Ratzinger presided over his funeral as Dean of the College of Cardinals. A couple of weeks later, the cardinal was elected Pope, taking the name of Pope Benedict XVI.

Within weeks of John Paul's death, people were calling for his sainthood—"*Santo subito!*" they would shout: Italian for "Sainthood now!" The beatification process, the first step in being named a saint, soon began.

Pope Benedict has been John Paul's most passionate pilgrim, and on May 1, 2011, he presided over the beatification of the late Pope before more than a million followers who crowded into St. Peter's Square and the surrounding streets.

Looking back at my coverage, I'm delighted to see with the clarity of time that I had witnessed something special, even if I didn't fully appreciate its significance in 1990. I had an inside glimpse into the relationship between these two reverent men and close friends—and without knowing it, an inside glimpse into the future of the Vatican.

—*James L. Stanfield*

Via della Conciliazione leads to St. Peter's Basilica and the larger-than-life-size Nativity aglow in the distance. The crèche, unveiled on Christmas Eve, was a popular tradition with visitors.

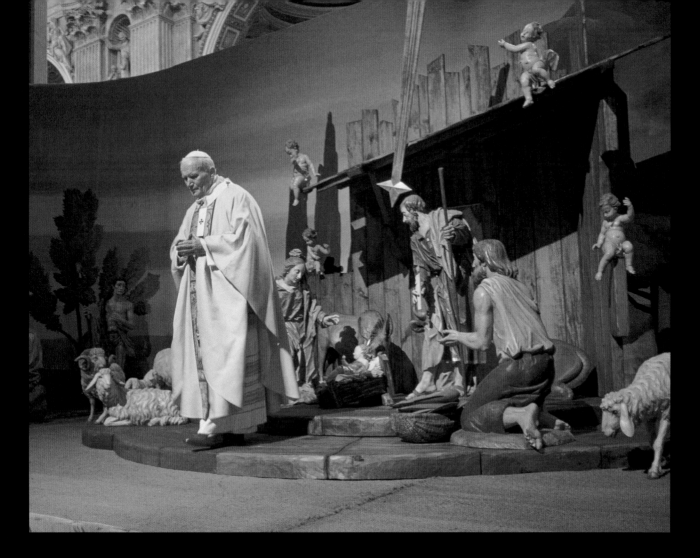

Toward the end of a Christmas Eve service in 1990, Pope John Paul II steps down from the life-size crèche near the baldachino *in St. Peter's Basilica. I took this photo just after he had blessed the entire Nativity scene.*

The Papacy of Pope Benedict

The far left entrance to St. Peter's Basilica is known as the Door of Death, the traditional pathway for Vatican funerals. It was refurbished in the 1960s with new bronze doors sculpted by Italian artist Giacomo Manzù, and it was through Manzù's ten-paneled relief that John Paul II was carried to his final rest on April 8, 2005. His simple cypress casket was turned to face some 300,000 gathered for a final goodbye in St. Peter's Square. John Paul had died six days earlier, closing a long and vibrant era for the Vatican. In more than 26 years, he had visited 129 countries beyond Italy, making him the most traveled Pope in history, as well as the third-longest-serving Pontiff.

The backdrop of those visits was one of extensive international change. The Berlin Wall fell and the Soviet Union disintegrated, liberating the church in John Paul's native Poland and helping advance reconciliation with Eastern Orthodoxy. He had made the first papal visit to key Jewish sites like the Wailing Wall in Jerusalem and was the first Pope to enter a Muslim house of worship. His tour of Syria's historic Umayyad Mosque in Damascus brought him to a structure that houses relics purported to be those of John the Baptist. In an adjacent garden stands the tomb of Muslim leader Saladin. The building served as a church in Christianity's early years. All of this helped show the continuity of faith around the world and emphasize John Paul's message of tolerance.

His travels also highlighted a growing sense that the church in an era of globalization faced a different set of challenges. While countries like China and India had long been world population centers, they were now becoming economic powers as well—ascendant on the world stage—with majority religious beliefs quite different from those of the Catholic Church's European core. Islam was expanding south in Africa, pushing east in Asia, and, with the collapse of Soviet

John Paul II's wide appeal was evident at his passing in 2005 as admirers gathered in St. Peter's Basilica and other Vatican sites to honor his life.

central authority, becoming noticeable as a force in Eastern Europe. Echoing more than a thousand years of division, Turkey's efforts to join the European Union were clouded by concern over admitting a majority Muslim and Asian country to the European grouping.

Pius X may have been the last Pope canonized, for his work at the start of the 20th century, but John Paul II is likely to get that status as well for steering the church into the complexities of the 21st. In fact, the process is well under way as John Paul's beatification took place May 1, 2011. Verification of one more miracle is needed for him to be declared a saint.

John Paul ushered in the e-mail era to the Vatican's top office—appropriate, perhaps, in light of his emphasis on opening new lines of communication with other communities of faith. Given that both population growth and church membership had stalled in many traditionally Catholic areas, he foresaw that the church had to present itself dynamically in parts of the world where the population is expanding.

*I*t has fallen to the former Cardinal Joseph Ratzinger to continue John Paul II's work, while putting his personal stamp on the church's 265th Pontificate. The cardinal emerged as a quick consensus choice when the College of Cardinals convened on April 18, 2005. The speed of their selection was noteworthy. Within about 24 hours, Ratzinger got the needed two-thirds majority among the 117 cardinals eligible to vote, in contrast to the multiweek conclaves that once preceded papal selection. That partly reflected Ratzinger's status as a key confidant to John Paul II. As the late Pope's hand-selected Prefect of the Congregation for the Doctrine of the Faith, Ratzinger for more than two decades had advised the church on doctrinal matters. In contrast to John Paul's peripatetic, almost missionary approach, Benedict emerged from an academic career that emphasized conservative values and Vatican authority, making him a favorite among traditionalists. He had served less than a year as a parish priest, but he was a well-known theologian, involved at the highest levels of church discourse since the Second Vatican Council in the early 1960s.

PRECEDING PAGES: Pope Benedict XVI greets the crowd in St. Peter's Square during the beatification ceremony for his predecessor, Pope John Paul II, on May 1, 2011. The former Cardinal Ratzinger was a trusted confidant of the late Pope.

He also had the advantage, perhaps, of appearing as a transitional figure. Ratzinger turned 78 just days before his election, making him the oldest Pope to take office since the 18th century. His age put him just two years shy of the cutoff for voting in a papal election, a restriction that John Paul II had instituted in an effort to streamline the often cumbersome process. After suffering a pair of minor strokes in the early 1990s, the cardinal had tried to retire, but John Paul II persuaded him to continue. After he was chosen Pope, Ratzinger joked that "the guillotine" had fallen on him—evidence of an understated wit, but also consistent with a yearning for a simpler life back in his native Bavaria.

His election came amid calls for a Pope from Africa or South America, developing regions that would better reflect the Catholic Church's majority membership and likely future growth. Catholic congregations are expanding along with the population in countries like Brazil, but are stagnating in Europe—a fact that focused attention on candidates like Brazilian Cardinal Claudio Hummes. Given the historical implications of electing the first Pope from outside Europe, Ratzinger offered continuity with the past without postponing change for decades more.

Ratzinger accepted the challenge, of course, and became Benedict XVI. He chose, in his papal name, to identify with a religious order that had expanded Christianity in Europe, and the name was consistent with his own hope for a moral revival on the increasingly secular continent. He had made clear when he was first tapped for a Vatican post in 1981 that service in Rome was God's career plan, not necessarily his own.

The future Pope spent his youth in a series of villages in Bavaria, an upbringing that left him with a love of the outdoors and of small-town, agrarian culture. His father was a police officer, his mother a baker and cook. His two siblings were close friends.

Benedict's childhood was steeped in traditional values and a traditional view of religion. Along with his family's strong ties to Catholicism—his parents were devout, one uncle was a priest and theologian, and his brother, Georg, was also ordained—the towns in which Benedict was raised helped inspire his spiritual imagination. The villages had roots in Celtic and Roman settlements, and the local churches reflected that history.

"I breathed the Baroque ever since I was a child," Benedict wrote in his memoir *Milestones,* referring to a youth spent worshipping in centuries-old sanctuaries that captured, for him, Catholicism's aura.

Benedict was born on April 16, 1927, in the small village of Marktl am Inn, a town of only 2,700 at the time, near the Austrian border. Born on Holy Saturday, the day before Easter, he was baptized the same day in St. Oswald's Church, with water blessed for the coming celebration. His family moved in 1929 to the nearby town of Tittmoning, and again in 1932 to Aschau am Inn, where they resided in an apartment provided at the local police station.

Five years later, they moved to Traunstein, a town that Benedict finally considered home, but in an era that would prove unsettling nonetheless. The Nazi Party's influence had been creeping deeper into small-town life, and by 1939 was an inescapable fact. As Benedict entered a local seminary, German tanks arrived in Prague and Poland. Within two years, he had been drawn into the Hitler Youth—an almost unavoidable obligation—and two years after that, began forced military service at an antiaircraft battery in Munich.

His service lasted until near the war's conclusion, with some of the final weeks spent on a largely make-work assignment back in Traunstein. Near the end, he deserted altogether, leaving the Nazi barracks for the refuge of his parents' home. When American troops arrived, he was rounded up like the other soldiers and taken to a camp near Ulm, where he was confined with tens of thousands awaiting the formal finish of the conflict. When that came on June 19, 1945, he made his way home, followed a month later by his brother Georg.

Though Benedict already had spent time in the seminary before war upended the country, more than 50 years later he would cite turmoil of the war years as central to his conviction that the church and priesthood were needed as a moral center. In Brennan Pursell's biography of the Pope, Benedict is quoted as telling a Canadian youth group in 2006 that, after hearing the anti-Catholic harangues of Nazi Party members, "I understood in confronting the brutality of this system, this inhuman face, that there is a need for priests, precisely as a contrast to this inhuman culture."

Benedict resumed his religious studies after the war at the seminary in Freising, but soon transferred to the University of Munich with the intent of immersing himself more in theology and academics than in the fieldwork of the priesthood. Following his ordination in June 1951, he did serve nearly a year at a parish in Munich, but within ten months he was appointed to the faculty of the Freising seminary—the formal start of an academic and intellectual career that would lead to the chair of St. Peter. He received his doctorate in 1953 and quickly won a name for himself among theologians, being tapped for a professorship at the University in Bonn and then brought on as a theological adviser at the Second Vatican Council.

The council and other events of the 1960s would prove critical to his thinking. Though supportive of the decisions made at Vatican II, he became uneasy with the more liberal slant given to the council's decisions as they were applied in churches and parishes around the world. As a faculty member at the University in Tübingen, Benedict watched the protest movements of the late 1960s unfold in a way that he felt distorted the teachings and practice of the church, bending Christianity into Marxist and other contortions. He probably needed little convincing, but the experience reemphasized his focus on the importance of maintaining the essence of the faith and the essence of its doctrine and practice.

"This is His Church, and not a laboratory for theologians" is how Benedict put it in his book *Salt of the Earth*. That same spirit guided his work under John Paul II as head of the Vatican office in charge of doctrinal issues, and has carried forward into his own term as Pope.

The symbols and garments that Benedict chose to inaugurate his ministry as Pope struck that same note of continuity.

As with the knights and royalty of the Middle Ages, it is common for ranking members of the clergy to choose a coat of arms and other items that speak to their history or priorities. In Benedict's case, the chasuble, or outer vestment, he donned for the Mass that began his Pontificate was decorated with a scallop-shell design. The Vatican's official website attributes triple significance to the insignia: first, Benedict, a student of Augustinian theology, knew St. Augustine's comparison of his own limitations in trying to understand God to a child trying to empty the ocean with a seashell; second, the shell is part of the heraldry of a monastery in Benedict's home region of Bavaria; and third, the shell, long a symbol of pilgrimage, pays homage to the travels of John Paul II and Benedict's hope to sustain a comparable outreach to the world.

The scallop shell is also the central image in Benedict's papal coat of arms, a design that can be read as a basic personal statement. Above the shell to the left is a Moor's head—a symbol of the ancient diocese of Freising and a reference to Benedict's deep Bavarian roots. To the right is a bear carrying a pack—a device that refers to the Bavarian legend of St. Corbinian taming a bear to do the duty of a slaughtered horse.

*I*t became apparent early in Benedict's tenure that his position as Pope differed from those jobs he had held before. The Congregation for the Doctrine of the Faith was well tailored to Benedict's literalist side, the aspect of his personality that reveled in theology and tradition. But as head of the church, his words took on amplified importance.

In a September 2006 address at the University of Regensburg, he learned just how intense the scrutiny would be. The largely academic speech—a discussion of rationality, science, and faith—included a passage from a medieval text that referred to the teachings of the Muslim Prophet Muhammad as "evil and inhumane." Though Benedict was referring to the text as part of a long discourse and was not endorsing that point of view the speech led to riots in some Muslim cities and extensive diplomatic fallout. The Vatican issued a series of clarifying statements, including Benedict's own apology for the confusion he had caused, while church analysts debated whether the Pope grasped the difference between his prior role as a pure theologian and his new one as diplomat to the world.

Benedict's decision in the summer of 2007 to allow wider use of the Latin Tridentine Mass stirred complaints among Jews because it contained a Good Friday prayer that called on God to lift Jews' "blindness" to Christ. The Latin rite had fallen into disuse after Vatican Council II, leading to a schism with some church traditionalists that Benedict hoped to heal.

In these two instances and others, the Pope showed he was adaptable—and not a captive of his academic convictions. The language of the Tridentine Good Friday prayer was modified to assuage the backlash among Jewish groups, and sensitivities in the Muslim world were addressed head-on when Benedict visited Turkey in November 2006.

That trip had been in danger of cancellation following the uproar over Benedict's speech at Regensburg. First conceived as outreach to the Orthodox Church, the visit instead focused on the Pope's edgy relations with the Islamic world. Over the course of four days, Benedict showed that he was sensitive to the grand gestures sometimes needed on the world stage. His arrival speech spoke of the "great esteem" he held for Muslims, but the more powerful moment came near the end of the visit, when he entered the Sultan Ahmet Mosque accompanied by Turkish religious leader Mustafa Cagrici. Removing his shoes in the customary fashion, Benedict strolled through the magnificent Blue Mosque with his host. When Cagrici paused for prayer and turned toward Mecca, Benedict joined him, a sign of respect and fraternity that caught the imagination of the Turkish people and press.

Benedict took on another thorny issue during his spring 2008 trip to the United States: sexual abuse by members of the Catholic clergy. For all his successes, John Paul II had not been as aggressive in dealing with this crisis as victims and their advocates would have liked. Benedict pushed the issue to the fore, beginning with comments to the press during his airplane trip across the Atlantic. After a Mass at Nationals Park in Washington, D.C., he met at the Vatican Embassy with five victims of clerical sexual abuse, holding individual conversations with each and joining in what was described as a highly emotional moment of prayer. The theme continued in a homily at New York's St. Patrick's Cathedral when he noted that the church was going through "a time of purification . . . and a time for healing." And while visiting Great Britain in September 2010—the first papal trip there since 1982—the Pontiff offered a strong critique of the Catholic Church's handling of the sex abuse crisis, saying the church had not been "sufficiently vigilant" or "sufficiently quick and decisive in taking the necessary measures."

Though Benedict took office under a banner of continuity with John Paul II, his outreach to the victims of sexual abuse has again shown a willingness to adjust—a trait that has become even more evident as his tenure advances. His increasingly strong denunciations of abuse are bringing some changes, and the Vatican has asked bishops around the world to come up with common guidelines to guard against pedophiles by spring 2012.

The Pope is also working to mend relations with the Jewish community. In March 2011, he visited Fosse Ardeatine, a cave near Rome where 335 Italians, many of whom were Jewish, were murdered in 1944. The trip commemorating the 67th anniversary of the massacre followed on the heels of Benedict's landmark statement exonerating Jews in the death of Jesus. In his recent book *Jesus of Nazareth, Part II,* he states that no theological basis exists in scripture for the argument that Jews as a whole were responsible for Jesus' crucifixion. Interpretations to the contrary have been used for centuries to justify persecution of the Jews, and Jewish scholars believe the argument presented by the German-born Pope will help fight anti-Semitism. By putting his personal stamp on the controversial issue, Benedict made it clear where he and the Vatican stand on the topic.

The church is an ancient institution, and its long-standing headquarters is the Vatican—a complex that serves unique religious, cultural, and diplomatic roles. Contemporary issues, however, such as climate change and the reality of limited resources, are likely to gain urgency in coming years, defining Benedict's time in office just as the reordering of the Soviet Union helped define John Paul's.

But in his initial encyclical, issued on Christmas of his first year in office, Benedict laid the groundwork for his Pontificate by harkening back both to his earliest years of scholarship and to his earliest faith in a caring God. "Deus Caritas Est" ("God Is Love") had the hallmarks of a philosophic treatise, delving into Greek etymology and Nietzsche's criticism of Christianity.

Yet Benedict was clear. Though an academic by training and perhaps by temperament, he wants his words to echo into action—"to call forth in the world," as he wrote, "renewed energy and commitment in the human response to God's love."

Benedict XVI, the former Cardinal Joseph Ratzinger, was elected Pope at the age of 78 in 2005. Before becoming Pope, he was one of the most influential men in the Roman Curia, the governing body of the Catholic Church.

Benedict XVI visits with Istanbul's Grand Mufti (opposite), Mustafa Cagrici, during a 2006 trip to Turkey. At the 500-year-old Sultan Ahmet Mosque, an Ottoman masterpiece also known as the Blue Mosque, Benedict faced Mecca in a prayer with the Grand Mufti. As a sign of respect, he doffed his shoes, as is customary when entering a Muslim house of worship. During the visit, the Pope reemphasized the urgency of tolerance in the world.

The Vatican serves as a seat of diplomacy as well as a center of religious activity. President Barack Obama (right) greeted the Holy Father in 2009, saying it was a "great honor" to meet the Pontiff. The two men discussed immigration policy, the Middle East, and aid to developing nations. In September 2010, Benedict traveled to Scotland to meet Queen Elizabeth II and Prince Philip at their Edinburgh residence, Holyrood House.

A detail of Benedict's garments (below) showcases an essential symbol of his office—the ring of the fisherman. The gold ring depicts St. Peter casting his fishing net and honors the Apostle as the first Pope. Each Pope selects a new ring, which is destroyed after his death. The Pope also wears a large cross, called a pectoral cross, suspended on a gold cord.

In March 2009, the Holy Father traveled to Angola (right) as part of a week-long trip to Africa. He held an outdoor Mass in Luanda during his stay in Angola, which was the first sub-Saharan African country to be evangelized by missionaries about 500 years ago. Benedict began his first visit to Africa as Pontiff by saying he was bringing the "Christian message of hope" to a continent ravaged by conflict, poverty, and AIDS.

In March 2011, Benedict visited Fosse Ardeatine, the site near Rome where 335 Italian men and boys, many of them Jews, were executed by Nazi troops in 1944. The act was a reprisal by the German troops for a partisan attack that had killed 33 of their comrades. The Italians were rounded up from houses, jails, and the streets. The Pope's visit commemorated the 67th anniversary of the executions, which the German-born Pope said were "a grave offense to God."

Benedict rose through the church's academic ranks, spending only one year as a parish priest. Yet the Holy Father has emphasized in his writing and sermons the central importance of the church's sacraments and rituals— the routines that the church's clergy administer. In January 2008, the Pope baptized one of a group of infants (opposite) in the Sistine Chapel for the Feast of the Epiphany, a tradition begun by Pope John Paul II.

The Holy Father glides through the canals of Venice (below) in the Dogaressa gondola, a boat styled for Venice's ancient rulers. The Pontiff spent two days in the area in May 2011 to highlight the Christian heritage of this crossroads of Mediterranean and Eastern European history. The boat is the same from which John Paul II greeted admirers along the Grand Canal in 1985.

*B*enedict holds the Paschal candle (below) as he celebrates the Easter Vigil in St. Peter's Basilica in 2009. The solemn, three-hour-plus ceremony—the first official celebration of the resurrection of Jesus—always occurs on the Saturday night before Easter. The Pope blesses the candle and carries it in a procession at the beginning of the service, which starts in complete darkness.

Priests from local dioceses attend the Mass of the Chrism in St. Peter's Basilica (right) on Holy Thursday, April 21, 2011. The priests come to the Mass to celebrate with their bishop—in this case, the Holy Father, Pope Benedict XVI, who is also the Bishop of Rome. During the Mass, clergy members renew their vows of holy orders.

An acrobatic cyclist performs for the Pope during a general audience in St. Peter's Square in October 2010. During these audiences, people from around the world gather to receive the Pope's blessing.

A historic center of U.S. Catholicism, St. Patrick's Cathedral in New York City (below) hosted its first papal mass during Benedict's 2008 trip. The Pope used the U.S. journey to address the issue of clerical sexual abuse. At St. Patrick's, the audience included mostly members of the clergy, and Benedict told them the scandal presented the church with "a time of purification . . . and a time for healing." At a rally at St. Joseph's Seminary the same day (right), future nuns and priests welcomed the Pontiff with banners and applause.

An immense drapery with an image of John Paul II is erected (left) for his beatification, which took place in the Vatican on May 1, 2011. More than a million people gathered in St. Peter's Square and neighboring streets for the event.

Pope Benedict XVI kneels before the casket of the Blessed John Paul II (right) in front of St. Peter's Basilica's high altar during his beatification. The late Pope's coffin had been removed from his tomb in the basilica's crypt for the ceremony. Verification of another miracle is needed for him to be declared a saint.

The Popes

St. Peter *(d. c. 64)*

St. Linus *(c. 66-c. 78)*

St. Anacletus *(c. 79-c. 91)*

St. Clement I *(c. 91-c. 101)*

St. Evaristus *(c. 100-c. 109)*

St. Alexander I *(c. 109-c. 116)*

St. Sixtus I *(c. 116-c. 125)*

St. Telesphorus *(c. 125-c. 136)*

St. Hyginus *(c. 138-c. 142)*

St. Pius I *(c. 142-c. 155)*

St. Anicetus *(c. 155-c. 166)*

St. Soter *(c. 166-c. 174)*

St. Eleutherius, or Eleutherus *(c. 174-89)*

St. Victor I *(189-98)*

St. Zephyrinus *(198/9-217)*

St. Callistus I *(often Calixtus) (217-22)*

St. Urban I *(222-30)*

St. Pontian *(21 July 230-28 Sept. 235)*

St. Anterus *(21 Nov. 235-3 Jan. 236)*

St. Fabian *(10 Jan. 236-20 Jan. 250)*

St. Cornelius *(Mar. 251-June 253)*

St. Lucius I *(25 June 253-5 Mar. 254)*

St. Stephen I *(12 May 254-2 Aug. 257)*

St. Sixtus II *(Aug. 257-6 Aug. 258)*

St. Dionysius *(22 July 260-26 Dec. 268)*

St. Felix I *(3 Jan. 269-30 Dec. 274)*

St. Eutychian *(4 Jan. 275-7 Dec. 283)*

St. Gaius, or Caius *(17 Dec. 283-22 Apr. 296)*

St. Marcellinus *(30 June 296-? 304; d. 25 Oct. 304)*

St. Marcellus I *(Nov./Dec. 306-16 Jan. 308)*

St. Eusebius *(18 Apr.-21 Oct. 310)*

St. Miltiades, or Melchiades *(2 July 311-10 Jan. 314)*

St. Silvester I *(31 Jan. 314-31 Dec. 335)*

St. Mark *(18 Jan.-7 Oct. 336)*

St. Julius I *(6 Feb. 337-12 Apr. 352)*

Liberius *(17 May 352-24 Sept. 366)*

St. Damasus I *(1 Oct. 366-11 Dec. 384)*

St. Siricius *(Dec. 384-26 Nov. 399)*

St. Anastasius I *(27 Nov. 399-19 Dec. 401)*

St. Innocent I *(21 Dec. 401-12 Mar. 417)*

St. Zosimus *(18 Mar. 417-26 Dec. 418)*

St. Boniface I *(28 Dec. 418-4 Sept. 422)*

St. Celestine I *(10 Sept. 422-27 July 432)*

St. Sixtus, or Xystus III *(31 July 432-19 Aug. 440)*

St. Leo I *(Aug./Sept. 440-10 Nov. 461)*

St. Hilarus *(19 Nov. 461-29 Feb. 468)*

St. Simplicius *(3 Mar. 468-10 Mar. 483)*

St. Felix III (II) *(13 Mar. 483-1 Mar. 492)*

St. Gelasius I *(1 Mar. 492-21 Nov. 496)*

Anastasius II *(24 Nov. 496-19 Nov. 498)*

St. Symmachus *(22 Nov. 498-19 July 514)*

St. Hormisdas *(20 July 514-6 Aug. 523)*

St. John I *(13 Aug. 523-18 May 526)*

St. Felix IV (III) *(12 July 526-22 Sept. 530)*

Boniface II *(22 Sept. 530-17 Oct. 532)*

John II *(2 Jan. 533-8 May 535)*

St. Agapitus I *(13 May 535-22 Apr. 536)*

St. Silverius *(8 June 536-11 Nov. 537; d. 2 Dec. 537)*

Vigilius *(29 Mar. 537-7 June 555)*

Pelagius I *(16 Apr. 556-3 Mar. 561)*

John III *(17 July 561-13 July 574)*

Benedict I *(2 June 575-30 July 579)*

Pelagius II *(26 Nov. 579-7 Feb. 590)*

St. Gregory I *(3 Sept. 590-12 Mar. 604)*

Sabinian *(13 Sept. 604-22 Feb. 606)*

Boniface III *(19 Feb.-12 Nov. 607)*

St. Boniface IV *(15 Sept. 608-8 May 615)*

St. Deusdedit (later Adeodatus I) *(19 Oct. 615-8 Nov. 618)*

Boniface V *(23 Dec. 619-25 Oct. 625)*

Honorius I *(27 Oct. 625-12 Oct. 638)*

Severinus *(28 May-2 Aug. 640)*

John IV *(24 Dec. 640-12 Oct. 642)*

Theodore I *(24 Nov. 642-14 May 649)*

St. Martin I *(5 July 649-17 June 653; d. 16 Sept. 655)*

St. Eugene I *(10 Aug. 654-2 June 657)*

St. Vitalian *(30 July 657-27 Jan. 672)*

Adeodatus II *(11 Apr. 672-17 June 676)*

Donus *(2 Nov. 676-11 Apr. 678)*

St. Agatho *(27 June 678-10 Jan. 681)*

St. Leo II *(17 Aug. 682-3 July 683)*

St. Benedict II *(26 June 684-8 May 685)*

John V *(23 July 685-2 Aug. 686)*

Conon *(21 Oct. 686-21 Sept. 687)*

St. Sergius I *(15 Dec. 687-9 Sept. 701)*

John VI *(30 Oct. 701-11 Jan. 705)*

John VII *(1 Mar. 705-18 Oct. 707)*

Sisinnius *(15 Jan.-4 Feb. 708)*

Constantine *(25 Mar. 708-9 Apr. 715)*

St. Gregory II *(19 May 715-11 Feb. 731)*

St. Gregory III *(18 Mar. 731-28 Nov. 741)*

St. Zacharias *(3 Dec. 741-15 Mar. 752)*

Stephen (II) *(22 or 23-25 or 26 Mar. 752)*

Stephen II (III) *(26 Mar. 752-26 Apr. 757)*

St. Paul I *(29 May 757-28 June 767)*

Stephen III (IV) *(7 Aug. 768-24 Jan. 772)*

Hadrian I *(1 Feb. 772-25 Dec. 795)*

St. Leo III *(26 Dec. 795-12 June 816)*

Stephen IV (V) *(22 June 816-24 Jan. 817)*

St. Paschal I *(24 Jan. 817-11 Feb. 824)*

Eugene II *(5? June 824-27? Aug. 827)*

Valentine *(Aug.-Sept. 827)*

Gregory IV *(late 827-25 Jan. 844)*

Sergius II *(Jan. 844-27 Jan. 847)*

St. Leo IV *(10 Apr. 847-17 July 855)*

Benedict III *(29 Sept. 855-17 Apr. 858)*

St. Nicholas I *(24 Apr. 858-13 Nov. 867)*

Hadrian II *(14 Dec. 867-Nov. or Dec. 872)*

John VIII *(14 Dec. 872-16 Dec. 882)*

Marinus I *(16 Dec. 882-15 May 884)*

St. Hadrian III *(17 May 884-mid-Sept. 885)*

Stephen V (VI) *(Sept. 885-14 Sept. 891)*

Formosus *(6 Oct. 891-4 Apr. 896)*

Boniface VI *(Apr. 896)*

Stephen VI (VII) *(May 896-Aug. 897)*

Romanus *(Aug.-Nov. 897; d. ?)*

Theodore II *(Nov. 897)*

John IX *(Jan. 898-Jan. 900)*

Benedict IV *(May/June 900-Aug. 903)*

Leo V *(Aug.-Sept. 903; d. early 904)*

Sergius III *(29 Jan. 904-14 Apr. 911)*

Anastasius III *(c. June 911-c. Aug. 913)*

Lando *(c. Aug. 913-c. Mar. 914)*

John X *(Mar./Apr. 914-deposed May 928; d. 929)*

Leo VI *(May-Dec. 928)*

Stephen VII (VIII) *(Dec. 928-Feb. 931)*

John XI *(Feb. or Mar. 931-Dec. 935 or Jan. 936)*

Leo VII *(3 Jan. 936-13 July 939)*

Stephen VIII (IX) *(14 July 939-late Oct. 942)*

Marinus II *(30 Oct. 942-early May 946)*

Agapitus II *(10 May 946-Dec. 955)*

John XII *(16 Dec. 955-14 May 964)*

Leo VIII *(4 Dec. 963-1 Mar. 965)*

Benedict V *(22 May-deposed 23 June 964; d. 4 July 966)*

John XIII *(1 Oct. 965-6 Sept. 972)*

Benedict VI *(19 Jan. 973-July 974)*

Benedict VII *(Oct. 974-10 July 983)*
John XIV *(Dec. 983-20 Aug. 984)*
John XV *(mid-Aug. 985-Mar. 996)*
Gregory V *(3 May 996-18 Feb. 999)*
Sylvester II *(2 Apr. 999-12 May 1003)*
John XVII *(16 May-6 Nov. 1003)*
John XVIII *(25 Dec. 1003-June or July 1009)*
Sergius IV *(31 July 1009-12 May 1012)*
Benedict VIII *(17 May 1012-9 Apr. 1024)*
John XIX *(19 Apr. 1024-20 Oct. 1032)*
Benedict IX *(21 Oct. 1032-Sept. 1044;*
    10 Mar.-1 May 1045; 8 Nov. 1047-
    16 July 1048; d. 1055/6)
Silvester III *(20 Jan.-10 Mar. 1045; d. 1063)*
Gregory VI *(1 May 1045-20 Dec. 1046;*
    d. late 1047)
Clement II *(24 Dec. 1046-9 Oct. 1047)*
Damasus II *(17 July-9 Aug. 1048)*
St. Leo IX *(12 Feb. 1049-19 Apr. 1054)*
Victor II *(13 Apr. 1055-28 July 1057)*
Stephen IX (X) *(2 Aug. 1057-29 Mar. 1058)*
Nicholas II *(6 Dec. 1058-19 or 26 July 1061)*
Alexander II *(30 Sept. 1061-21 Apr. 1073)*
St. Gregory VII *(22 Apr. 1073-25 May 1085)*
Bl. Victor III *(24 May 1086; 9 May-*
    16 Sept. 1087)
Bl. Urban II *(12 Mar. 1088-29 July 1099)*
Paschal II *(13 Aug. 1099-21 Jan. 1118)*
Gelasius II *(24 Jan. 1118-29 Jan. 1119)*
Callistus II *(2 Feb. 1119-14 Dec. 1124)*
Celestine (II) *(15/16 Dec. 1124; d. 1125/6)*
Honorius II *(21 Dec. 1124-13 Feb. 1130)*
Innocent II *(14 Feb. 1130-24 Sept. 1143)*
Celestine II *(26 Sept. 1143-8 Mar. 1144)*
Lucius II *(12 Mar. 1144-15 Feb. 1145)*
Bl. Eugene III *(15 Feb. 1145-8 July 1153)*
Anastasius IV *(8 July 1153-3 Dec. 1154)*
Hadrian IV *(4 Dec. 1154-1 Sept. 1159)*
Alexander III *(7 Sept. 1159-30 Aug. 1181)*
Lucius III *(1 Sept. 1181-25 Nov. 1185)*
Urban III *(25 Nov. 1185-19/20 Oct. 1187)*
Gregory VIII *(21 Oct.-17 Dec. 1187)*
Clement III *(19 Dec. 1187-late Mar. 1191)*
Celestine III *(Mar./Apr. 1191-8 Jan. 1198)*
Innocent III *(8 Jan. 1198-16 July 1216)*
Honorius III *(18 July 1216-18 Mar. 1227)*
Gregory IX *(19 Mar. 1227-22 Aug. 1241)*
Celestine IV *(25 Oct.-10 Nov. 1241)*

Innocent IV *(25 June 1243-7 Dec. 1254)*
Alexander IV *(12 Dec. 1254-25 May 1261)*
Urban IV *(29 Aug. 1261-2 Oct. 1264)*
Clement IV *(5 Feb. 1265-29 Nov. 1268)*
Bl. Gregory X *(1 Sept. 1271-10 Jan. 1276)*
Bl. Innocent V *(21 Jan.-22 June 1276)*
Hadrian V *(11 July-18 Aug. 1276)*
John XXI *(8 Sept. 1276-20 May 1277)*
Nicholas III *(25 Nov. 1277-22 Aug. 1280)*
Martin IV *(22 Feb. 1281-28 Mar. 1285)*
Honorius IV *(2 Apr. 1285-3 Apr. 1287)*
Nicholas IV *(22 Feb. 1288-4 Apr. 1292)*
St. Peter Celestine V *(5 July-13 Dec. 1294;*
    d. 19 May 1296)
Boniface VIII *(24 Dec. 1294-11 Oct. 1303)*
Bl. Benedict XI *(22 Oct. 1303-7 July 1304)*
Clement V *(5 June 1305-20 Apr. 1314)*
John XXII *(7 Aug. 1316-4 Dec. 1334)*
Benedict XII *(20 Dec. 1334-25 Apr. 1342)*
Clement VI *(7 May 1342-6 Dec. 1352)*
Innocent VI *(18 Dec. 1352-12 Sept. 1362)*
Bl. Urban V *(28 Sept. 1362-19 Dec. 1370)*
Gregory XI *(30 Dec. 1370-27 Mar. 1378)*
Urban VI *(8 Apr. 1378-15 Oct. 1389)*
Boniface IX *(2 Nov. 1389-1 Oct. 1404)*
Innocent VII *(17 Oct. 1404-6 Nov. 1406)*
Gregory XII *(30 Nov. 1406-4 July 1415;*
    d. 18 Oct. 1417)
Martin V *(11 Nov. 1417-20 Feb. 1431)*
Eugene IV *(3 Mar. 1431-23 Feb. 1447)*
Nicholas V *(6 Mar. 1447-24 Mar. 1455)*
Callistus III *(8 Apr. 1455-6 Aug. 1458)*
Pius II *(19 Aug. 1458-15 Aug. 1464)*
Paul II *(30 Aug. 1464-26 July 1471)*
Sixtus IV *(9 Aug. 1471-12 Aug. 1484)*
Innocent VIII *(29 Aug. 1484-25 July 1492)*
Alexander VI *(11 Aug. 1492-18 Aug. 1503)*
Pius III *(22 Sept.-18 Oct. 1503)*
Julius II *(1 Nov. 1503-21 Feb. 1513)*
Leo X *(11 Mar. 1513-1 Dec. 1521)*
Hadrian VI *(9 Jan. 1522-14 Sept. 1523)*
Clement VII *(19 Nov. 1523-25 Sept. 1534)*
Paul III *(13 Oct. 1534-10 Nov. 1549)*
Julius III *(8 Feb. 1550-23 Mar. 1555)*
Marcellus II *(9 Apr.-1 May 1555)*
Paul IV *(23 May 1555-18 Aug. 1559)*
Pius IV *(25 Dec. 1559-9 Dec. 1565)*
St. Pius V *(7 Jan. 1566-1 May 1572)*

Gregory XIII *(14 May 1572-10 Apr. 1585)*
Sixtus V *(24 Apr. 1585-27 Aug. 1590)*
Urban VII *(15-27 Sept. 1590)*
Gregory XIV *(5 Dec. 1590-16 Oct. 1591)*
Innocent IX *(29 Oct.-30 Dec. 1591)*
Clement VIII *(30 Jan. 1592-5 Mar. 1605)*
Leo XI *(1-27 Apr. 1605)*
Paul V *(16 May 1605-28 Jan. 1621)*
Gregory XV *(9 Feb. 1621-8 July 1623)*
Urban VIII *(6 Aug. 1623-29 July 1644)*
Innocent X *(15 Sept. 1644-1 Jan. 1655)*
Alexander VII *(7 Apr. 1655-22 May 1667)*
Clement IX *(20 June 1667-9 Dec. 1669)*
Clement X *(29 Apr. 1670-22 July 1676)*
Bl. Innocent XI *(21 Sept. 1676-12 Aug. 1689)*
Alexander VIII *(6 Oct. 1689-1 Feb. 1691)*
Innocent XII *(12 July 1691-27 Sept. 1700)*
Clement XI *(23 Nov. 1700-19 Mar. 1721)*
Innocent XIII *(8 May 1721-7 Mar. 1724)*
Benedict XIII *(29 May 1724-21 Feb. 1730)*
Clement XII *(12 July 1730-6 Feb. 1740)*
Benedict XIV *(17 Aug. 1740-3 May 1758)*
Clement XIII *(6 July 1758-2 Feb. 1769)*
Clement XIV *(19 May 1769-*
    22 Sept. 1774)
Pius VI *(15 Feb. 1775-29 Aug. 1799)*
Pius VII *(14 Mar. 1800-20 July 1823)*
Leo XII *(28 Sept. 1823-10 Feb. 1829)*
Pius VIII *(31 Mar. 1829-30 Nov. 1830)*
Gregory XVI *(2 Feb. 1831-1 June 1846)*
Bl. Pius IX *(16 June 1846-7 Feb. 1878)*
Leo XIII *(20 Feb. 1878-20 July 1903)*
St. Pius X *(4 Aug. 1903-20 Aug. 1914)*
Benedict XV *(3 Sept. 1914-22 Jan. 1922)*
Pius XI *(6 Feb. 1922-10 Feb. 1939)*
Pius XII *(2 Mar. 1939-9 Oct. 1958)*
Bl. John XXIII *(28 Oct. 1958-3 June 1963)*
Paul VI *(21 June 1963-6 Aug. 1978)*
John Paul I *(26 Aug.-28 Sept. 1978)*
Bl. John Paul II *(16 Oct. 1978-2 Apr. 2005)*
Benedict XVI *(19 Apr. 2005-)*

Source: J. N. D. Kelly, *The Oxford Dictionary of Popes, 1986*

Index

Inside the Vatican

BY BART MCDOWELL
PHOTOGRAPHED BY JAMES L. STANFIELD

Published by the National Geographic Society

John M. Fahey, *Chairman of the Board and Chief Executive Officer*

Timothy T. Kelly, *President*

Declan Moore, *Executive Vice President; President, Publishing*

Melina Gerosa Bellows, *Executive Vice President; Chief Creative Officer, Books, Kids, and Family*

Prepared by the Book Division

Barbara Brownell Grogan, *Vice President and Editor in Chief*

Jonathan Halling, *Design Director, Books and Children's Publishing*

Marianne R. Koszorus, *Design Director, Books*

Lisa Thomas, *Senior Editor*

R. Gary Colbert, *Production Director*

Jennifer Thornton, *Managing Editor*

Meredith C. Wilcox, *Administrative Director, Illustrations*

Staff for This Edition

Barbara Payne, *Project Editor*

Stephen St. John, *Illustrations Editor*

Cinda Rose, *Designer*

Marjorie Weeke, *Editorial Consultant*

Susan Straight, *Contributing Editor*

Judith Klein, *Production Editor*

Cameron Zotter, *Design Assistant*

Staff for 2008 Edition

Jane Menyawi, *Project Editor & Illustrations Editor*

Sanaa Akkach, *Designer*

Howard Schneider, *Contributing Writer*

Richard Wain, *Production Project Manager*

Robert Waymouth, *Illustrations Specialist*

Staff for First Edition

Charles Kogod, *Project Editor & Illustrations Editor*

Elizabeth L. Newhouse, *Text Editor*

Jody Bolt, *Art Director*

Barbara A. Payne, *Research Editor*

Rebecca Lescaze, *Researcher*

Mary B. Dickinson, Leslie Allen, *Picture Legend Writers*

Richard Wain, *Production Project Manager*

Manufacturing and Quality Management

Christopher A. Liedel, *Chief Financial Officer*

Phillip L. Schlosser, *Senior Vice President*

Chris Brown, *Technical Director*

Nicole Elliott, *Manager*

Rachel Faulise, *Manager*

Robert L. Barr, *Manager*

The National Geographic Society is one of the world's largest nonprofit scientific and educational organizations. Founded in 1888 to "increase and diffuse geographic knowledge," the Society's mission is to inspire people to care about the planet. It reaches more than 400 million people worldwide each month through its official journal, *National Geographic,* and other magazines; National Geographic Channel; television documentaries; music; radio; films; books; DVDs; maps; exhibitions; live events; school publishing programs; interactive media; and merchandise. National Geographic has funded more than 9,600 scientific research, conservation and exploration projects and supports an education program promoting geographic literacy. For more information, visit www.nationalgeographic.com

For more information, please call 1-800-NGS LINE (647-5463) or write to the following address:
National Geographic Society
1145 17th Street N.W.
Washington, D.C. 20036-4688 U.S.A.

For information about special discounts for bulk purchases, please contact National Geographic Books Special Sales: ngspecsales@ngs.org

For rights or permissions inquiries, please contact National Geographic Books Subsidiary Rights: ngbookrights@ngs.org

ISBN: 978-1-4262-0917-8
ISBN: 978-1-4262-0918-5 (Deluxe)

The Library of Congress has cataloged the 2008 edition of this book as follows:
Library of Congress Cataloging-in-Publication Data

McDowell, Bart.
  Inside the Vatican / by Bart McDowell ; photographed by James L. Stanfield ; prepared by the Book Division, National Geographic Society.
      p. cm.
    Revision of the 1991 ed.
    Includes index.
    ISBN 978-1-4262-0443-2 (regular/hardcover)
  1. Vatican City--Description and travel. 2. Vatican City--Pictorial works. 3. Papacy.
I. Stanfield, James L. II. National Geographic Society (U.S.). Book Division III. Title.
  DG794.M35 2008
  945.6' 34--dc22

                      2008041988

Printed in the United States of America
11/RRDW-CML/1

Illustrations Credits

All photographs are by James L. Stanfield, with the exception of the following:
Front matter: ©Emanuela De Meo/CATHOLICPRESSPHOTO (Benedict in red papal hat); Servizio Fotografico L'Osservatore Romano (Pope blessing young boy).
The Legacy of Peter: Scala/Art Resource, N.Y. (24, 52); © NGS painting by Harry Bliss (36-7); Vatican Museums (48-9, 49); National Geographic Photographer Victor R. Boswell, Jr. (53, 54-5).
The Treasures: National Geographic Photographer Victor R. Boswell, Jr. (142, 176-7, 178-9); Nippon Television Network Corporation (144-5, 172-3); Vatican Museums (164, 164-5, 166-7, 168, 169 all, 170-1, 174, 174-5, 180, 183).
The Papacy of Pope Benedict: Gianni Giansanti/Gratzia Neri (228); ©Alessia Giuliani/CATHOLIC-PRESSPHOTO (230-231); Servizio Fotografico L'Osservatore Romano (239); AFP/Pool/Getty Images (240); ©CATHOLICPRESSPHOTO/Pool (241 up); Servizio Fotografico L'Osservatore Romano (241 low); ©Piotr Spalek/CATHOLICPRESSPHOTO (242); Grzegorz Galazka (242-243); ©OR/CATHOLICPRESSPHOTO (244-245); Franco Origlia/Getty Images (246); ©Alessandro Serranò/CATHOLICPRESSPHOTO (247); ©Alessia Giuliani/CATHOLICPRESSPHOTO (248); Servizio Fotografico L'Osservatore Romano (248-249); ©Katarzyna Artymiak/CATHOLIC-PRESSPHOTO (250-251); Brian Zak/SipaPress (252); Joachim Ladefoged/VII (252-253); ©Giancarlo Giuliani/CATHOLICPRESSPHOTO (254); ©CATHOLICPRESSPHOTO/Pool (255).